A PLACE
TO HIDE

A PLACE
TO HIDE

by Jayne Pettit

**MACMILLAN
CHILDREN'S BOOKS**

First published 1993 in USA by Scholastic Inc.

This edition published 1994 by Macmillan Children's Books
a division of Macmillan Publishers Limited
Cavaye Place London SW10 9PG
and Basingstoke

Associated companies throughout the world

ISBN 0 330 33893 5

3 5 7 9 8 6 4 2

A CIP catalogue record for this book is available
from the British Library

Phototypeset by Intype, London
Printed and bound in Great Britain by
Cox & Wyman Ltd, Reading, Berkshire

Contents

Acknowledgments

Diana Stein, Associate Director of the Jewish Foundation for Christian Rescuers/Anti-Defamation League (ADL), has given me countless hours of her time during the past two years, assisting me in my research, uncovering hundreds of stories about the rescuers, and verifying information about those whose experiences I eventually chose to tell. During that time, the foundation has located thousands of Christian rescuers and come to the aid of many who are now in need of medical and financial assistance.

I am grateful for the advice and suggestions given me by Dr Frances Sonnenschein, National Educational Director of the ADL; Dr Eva Fogelman, consultant to the Foundation and director of the Rescuer Project; the Reverend Douglas K. Huneke;

Rabbi Harold M. Schulweis, founder of the Jewish Foundation for Christian Rescuers; and to Abraham H. Foxman, National Director of the ADL for his foreword to this book.

Throughout the writing of *A Place to Hide*, Barrie Van Dyck, Ann Reit, and Amy Scheinberg have been generous in their encouragement and understanding, and my husband, Bin Pettit, gave me the support to continue what was, on more than one occasion, a very painful undertaking.

It is my hope that this account of the rescuers and their 'conspiracy of goodness' will serve as a tribute to all those remarkable people who, in Abraham Foxman's words, 'seemed to be ordinary people living typical lives, but each was blessed with a touch of greatness.'

The Jewish Foundation estimates that the number of rescuers ranges from fifty thousand to five hundred thousand. The stories that follow are only a few.

Jayne Pettit
Quechee, Vermont

Foreword

As a survivor of the Holocaust – a hidden child – I find special meaning in this book. As I read it, I felt that I was reading about myself, for my story could very well have been included among those it recounts in faithful detail.

Without a doubt, I am alive today because of the bravery of a Christian woman who, like the rescuers depicted in the following pages, risked her life to save a Jewish child. Reading this book brought my own experience home to me even more vividly and graphically.

Thanks to rescuers like her, two million children survived who, otherwise, would have perished with their mothers, fathers, sisters and brothers in the dark Hitlerian night simply because of the faith into which they were born.

As one of those fortunate ones, I have often wondered about the rescuers. What made them behave as they did when so many others either joined in the slaughter or pretended it was not happening?

I know the woman who rescued me has always been an example to me. There can be no better role models than the rescuers. They seemed to be ordinary people living typical lives, but each was blessed with a touch of greatness.

Abraham H. Foxman
National Director,
Anti-Defamation League

A Place
to Hide

Introduction

Once, not very long ago, a nightmare descended upon the face of Europe. Between the years 1933 and 1945, six million Jews were murdered. How could this have happened? And why?

The seeds of this horror were sown in ancient times, when Jews were ridiculed and looked upon as outcasts. In many countries, they couldn't own property or hold public office. By the time of Columbus's voyages to the New World, Jews were not even allowed to live in England, France, or Spain.

Throughout the centuries, anti-Semitism – or hatred of the Jews – continued. Then, during the years following World War I, Jews in Germany were blamed for many of the troubles that were happening in their country.

Soon, there appeared on the scene a young Austrian, an anti-Semite with dreams of a new Germany – a Third Reich, or empire, as he called it – led by an Aryan race cleansed of all people he considered inferior. The man's name was Adolf Hitler.

Year by year, Hitler's influence continued to grow. Soon, he was the undisputed spokesman of a new political group called the National Socialist German Workers' Party, or the 'Nazis'. By 1930, Hitler and his followers had won seats in the Reichstag, or parliament.

Once in power, Hitler moved quickly. Arrests and executions of thousands of political opponents occurred. Unions were crushed and civil rights abandoned. Newspapers and radio stations were seized, books were burned, and teachers throughout the country were ordered to teach the Nazi propaganda.

During the years between 1939 and 1944, Hitler's armies swept through Europe, and millions of Jews found themselves trapped by the onslaught of the German armies. This was a time of suffering, betrayal, and despair.

Yet, in the midst of this horror, there were in each country men and women who could not ignore the cries of human beings asking for nothing more than a place to hide and something to eat. In Germany, and later in countries throughout Europe, there were people who refused to ignore the pleas of thousands of Jews seeking help. For each rescuer, discovery would mean torture and certain death, and thousands did die.

Why then did these rescuers risk their lives and those of their families to save the men, women, and children of the Holocaust? Perhaps the answer lies in the question often asked by the rescuers themselves: *What would you have done?*

1
Miep

Twenty-four-year-old Miep Santrouschitz made her way through the bustling traffic of the early-morning rush hour. Pedalling vigorously, she wove her old black bicycle in and out of the push-carts and hordes of other office workers on bicycles heading for the business centre of Amsterdam. As she gained speed, her skirt billowed out behind her and her stomach tied into little knots. Turning onto a winding street lined with stately old trees and rows of gabled office buildings, Miep's mind raced. What would Otto Frank be like? Would he be impressed with her? Would she get the job?

The year was 1933 and times were hard. Holland, like other countries around the world, was caught in the grips of the Depression. Many people were unemployed, prices were soaring, and things were scarce. Miep had not worked for months, having lost her previous job in a company layoff. She was anxious about the interview she was about to have.

Glancing down at the news clipping squeezed between her handlebar and the palm of her hand, she read the address once more: N.Z. Voorburgwal 120–126.

Miep pedalled on until she arrived at number 120. Then, pushing her bike into one of the kerbside stalls, she quickly smoothed down her light-brown hair and entered the building. Somewhere at the back of her mind lay the feeling that today was going to be an important one. Little did she know how important it would really be.

Much to her delight, Miep got the job that Monday morning in 1933. She and Otto Frank, the Amsterdam head of Travies and Company – a small manufacturing firm based in Cologne, Germany – got on well during the interview, and she was immediately hired. During the months that followed, the two discovered they had much in common, for both Miep and Otto Frank were refugees. She from Austria at the end of World War I, and he, a recently arrived Jew from Hitler's Nazi Germany. Occasionally, during free moments, Otto would speak of his family and of his hopes for their safe arrival in Amsterdam one day soon. A kindly, shy man, Otto Frank had lived in Frankfurt and was a member of an important Jewish family that had been active in the business and banking community for many years. He had served as an army officer during World War I. Otto and Miep held long discussions about their fears for German Jews living in the shadow of Hitler. Surely Otto's wife and two little girls would be safer in Holland, where Jews had been a part of society for centuries.

One day, as Miep pored over a set of order forms on her desk, a quietly dressed woman in her thirties walked into the offices of Travies and Company. With her was a beautiful little girl of about four with enormous black eyes and a head full of shiny, dark-brown hair. Hearing their footsteps as they approached, Otto Frank left his desk and moved quickly to the door to greet the two visitors. Then turning to Miep, he proudly introduced his wife, Edith Frank-Hollander, and the younger of his two daughters, Anne. Margot, the couple's older daughter, was attending her first classes at an Amsterdam school, Otto explained.

As the years passed, thousands of Jews fled from Germany. Those who did not, or could not, were soon to be arrested, deported, and shipped to the first of Germany's concentration camps, Dachau and Buchenwald. More and more Jewish refugees sought freedom in Holland and many of them settled in Amsterdam. Among these were Herman Van Daan and his wife, Petronella. Van Daan soon joined the firm of Travies and Company, which was by now prospering and expanding.

Miep, meanwhile, had begun dating Henk Gies, a Dutch social worker. Henk and Miep shared many interests, and the two young people took long walks on their lunch hours, talking in earnest about Hitler's growing power.

Miep and Henk were frequent dinner guests of Otto Frank and his family. The Franks' daughters were always present – Margot, quiet and studious, and Anne, bubbly, chatty, and intensely curious about everything. Both girls were by now students at the Montessori school, where Margot excelled in all subjects, and Anne, ever enthusiastic and eager for fun, had made many good friends. At the close of the evening meal, after the girls had returned to their studies, conversation immediately turned to the events unfolding in Germany.

On one such evening, the four adults spoke in hushed tones of the devastation that had just taken place throughout Germany as thousands of shops and businesses were smashed and hundreds of homes and synagogues were robbed, looted, and torn apart. Twenty-eight thousand people were sent to concentration camps, while another thousand were murdered. The massacre became known as *Kristallnacht* – the Night of Broken Glass. The year was 1938. Hitler and his armies had advanced into the Rhineland, Austria, and parts of Czechoslovakia.

By 1939, while the rest of the world ignored the German threat, Hitler, ever more confident in the face of the almost total lack of resistance to his advances, marched into Poland. By spring of the following year, the Germans had invaded defenceless

Denmark and its northern neighbour, Norway. The Netherlands would be next.

On a spring night in May of 1940, while most of the people of Amsterdam were asleep, the drone of airplanes was heard across the skies. Gradually, in house after house across the city, lights flashed on and the faces of anxious residents appeared at their windows.

In the little house in the River Quarter of South Amsterdam, Catherina Santrouschitz sprang out of her bed and crossed the room toward the bed where her stepsister Miep tossed in a restless sleep. Shaking Miep vigorously, Catherina told her to get up. Something terrible was happening, she cried. Something the people of Holland had dreaded for months.

The two young women threw on their robes and made their way down the darkened stairway to the small living room where their parents had gathered around the radio. After some time, a voice came through heavy static to announce the news that everyone already knew: The Germans were attacking.

Five days later, on 15 May 1940, as the city of Rotterdam lay in ruins, the courageous Dutch Resistance forces crumbled in the face of the enemy's overwhelming strength. Soon, thousands of German soldiers goose-stepped victoriously along Dam Square in Amsterdam. Behind them rattled a convoy of armoured trucks and the thunder of tanks, crawling past a silent crowd of Dutch citizens.

During the next three days, the scene was repeated in Belgium and tiny Luxembourg, and finally, on the twenty-second of June, the Nazis seized control of France and hoisted the swastika to the top of the Eiffel Tower in Paris. It seemed the Germans could not lose.

Holland's invaders lost no time in making sweeping changes. As spring turned into summer, radio broadcasts announced the arrival of the new German Reichskommissar, movie houses showed only German films, and books the Germans had blacklisted disappeared from the shelves of schools, libraries, and shops. On street corners and in coffeehouses, the people gathered in clusters, exchanging whispered reports of the day's latest events. Everywhere, there was an air of fear. Holland was no longer free.

By the autumn of 1940, as the German Luftwaffe carried out its relentless bombing raids over Britain, all the Jews in Holland who held government jobs or public positions, schoolteachers, and university professors were ordered to resign. Businesses managed by Jewish partners were required to register at the offices of the Reichskommissar. Although Otto Frank and Herman Van Daan showed no visible concern about this turn of events, Miep and others working for Travies and Company, including Victor Kraler – a partner and a Gentile – voiced their anxieties. How could these things happen in Holland?

During the following months, posters reading

9

JEWS NOT WANTED HERE sprang up in public places, and the Jewish Quarter became a sealed ghetto. In February, four hundred men were seized in a round-up and deported to Mauthausen, a new concentration camp in Austria.

As these events took place, Miep and Henk, now married, worried about their Jewish friends, the Franks and the Van Daans. They were particularly frightened for Margot and Anne, who had been ordered out of the Montessori school and forced to attend an all-Jewish school. Overnight, Anne – now almost twelve – seemed older, showing her concern and her anger over the control the Nazis held over the Jews. Margot was now frequently ill, missing school, and growing increasingly pale and thin.

Days stretched into weeks and the weeks into months. More and more Jews were deported to forced labour camps in Germany and Poland. And in the final insult of all, Jews were required to wear a large, yellow Star of David on the fronts and backs of their clothing. Most of those who protested or refused, disappeared.

Then, during the late spring of 1942, Otto Frank called Miep into his office. Entering, she heard Frank locking the door behind her. Turning her head to take note of his unusual behaviour, she looked into Otto's face. Miep was suddenly frightened by the appearance of the quiet, serious man walking back to his desk.

Minutes passed, and then Frank began to speak. He feared for his wife and his two daughters. What would become of them if he were seized by the Germans? Where would they go? Then, Otto broke the terrible news. Margot had been ordered to report to a forced labour camp in Germany. Something had to be done immediately.

Step by step, Frank revealed the plans he had been making for months without his family's knowledge. Unable to flee the city, trapped and defenceless, the Franks, along with the Van Daans, were going into hiding. Would Miep help? Without hesitating for a moment, Miep assured Otto that she would, despite the dangers she'd face. Both she and Otto were aware of the edict that ordered death by hanging to Jews and those who assisted them in any effort to escape or to hide.

Dropping his voice to a whisper, Otto Frank disclosed the whereabouts of the hiding place. It was to be the Annexe, a series of rooms on several floors in the back of the building in which Travies and Company was situated. Secluded from the street and hidden by a giant chestnut tree, the Annexe would offer the only hope the Franks and the Van Daans held for survival. For weeks now, Otto and Herman had carried what few belongings they could gather for the life they and their families were about to begin. Books, sheets, blankets, towels, and canned foods – all had been silently hauled, bit by bit, to the rooms tucked secretly behind the company's offices. Miep was amazed at what the two men had accomplished before the very eyes of the workers, as well as the Green Police (who collaborated with the

Germans) and the Nazis, who scoured the homes, streets, and blocks of the city, searching for their next victims.

On the night before the two families were to go into hiding, Miep and Henk put on old raincoats, loose-fitting and long, with many pockets. They rode their bikes to the Franks' apartment where they filled their pockets with as many things as they could handle, stuffing whatever else they could inside the fronts of their tightly buttoned clothing. They made several trips to the Annexe and back, using darkened side streets and alleys. At curfew time, Miep and Henk returned to their own apartment.

The following morning, Miep pedalled quickly to the Franks' home, thankful that the pouring rain had driven most of the Green Police from the streets. When she arrived at her friends' home, Margot – ashen and silent – emerged from the doorway pushing her forbidden bicycle down the short steps in front of the building. Without speaking, the two quickly boarded their bikes and sped away, Miep in front with her briefcase resting in her basket, Margot in the rear with her schoolbag. The perfect picture of a mother and daughter heading for office and school with a busy day ahead. Margot had removed the yellow Stars of David from her clothing so as not to attract notice.

Arriving at the Travies offices, Miep and Margot hurried inside, moving quietly down the corridors and up the steps that led to the hidden Annexe. Opening the door to the entranceway and glancing furtively about her, Miep stepped aside while Margot slipped inside, closing the door to the world she had known for sixteen years.

Later in the day, after the office workers had left the building, Otto – accompanied by his wife and Anne – climbed the same steps, trying with all the strength they had not to think about the lives they were leaving behind.

On Wednesday, 8 July 1942, Anne Frank – now thirteen years old, opened the pages of the little checkered diary her father had given her for her birthday a month before and began her first entry since the Frank family had gone into hiding:

> Years seem to have passed between Sunday
> and now. So much has happened, it is just
> as if the world had turned upside down.
> But I am still alive . . . and that is the main
> thing, Daddy says.

For everyone, hiding meant no further communication with the outside world. From now on, there was just the little radio Otto had smuggled into their quarters. They would see the Travies staff – Miep and Henk and Elli Vossen from the offices downstairs, and Victor Kraler and Jo Koophuis, Otto Frank's business partners who had been told of the hiding place. These few would provide the only link with life as it once was.

At the end of that first day, Miep Gies waited until

the last of the office workers had gone home. Then, after making sure no one else was in the building, she walked along the hallway leading to the steps that led upstairs to the Annexe. As she made her way to the top of the stairs, she felt overwhelmed. How, she wondered, would these people manage in such a place? How would they fill the endless hours? And what would happen if one of them took sick? They could not call a doctor or a rabbi to comfort them or relatives.

Miep did her best to hide her fears as she looked at the four people who stood facing her. Quietly she reassured them that she would be there always, no matter what they might need.

She would come every day, she promised. She would be there early every morning, before any of the workers arrived downstairs, and at noon-time when everyone had left to have lunch, and at the close of the day. They were to tell her of any household problems, any medicines or supplies they needed. Each day, she would take their food list and, using the ration stamps of the people in Frank's company, bring back whatever she could find at the local markets. This, Miep realized, would be one of her most difficult tasks – for there was a limit to what she could carry – and soon she would be shopping for eight people. Miep worried about how she would be able to avoid suspicion buying large quantities of food, when it was known in the neighbourhood shops that she was a newly married woman. Shouldn't she just be shopping for two?

14

During the weeks that followed, Herman Van Daan, his wife, Petronella, and their son, Peter, joined the Franks in their hiding place. Later, room was made for Dr Albert Dussel, a dentist and a German refugee. His arrival meant less room for everyone in the already cramped quarters, as well as another mouth to feed. All, nevertheless, were deeply thankful that they had a place to hide and beds in which to sleep.

As each family settled into some kind of routine, they agreed on a set of rules. Since there was to be no signs of life in their rooms, they could do nothing that would arouse suspicion in the workers downstairs, neighbours in the adjoining office buildings, people walking on the pavements below, or Nazis patrolling the streets. They could make no sound while anyone was in the building. They couldn't wear shoes during the day, or flush a toilet, or use water for bathing or laundering. Speaking above a whisper or use of the radio was forbidden. Their cooking was limited to later evening hours so that smells from the kitchen and the sounds of pots and pans wouldn't betray them. There could be no air from open windows to rustle the thick curtains and blackout sheets. They couldn't turn on lights to read by on a dark day, or sneeze, cough, or scrape chairs on the bare floors. And above all, no figures could be seen moving behind the window curtains.

Each day, Miep climbed the stairs to the Annexe, bringing with her news from the outside world. Knowing how much these visits meant to everyone,

15

she chose her news with care, telling them of friends who had managed to find shelter, or of the progress of Travies and Company, or any encouraging news about the war.

What Miep did *not* speak of were the increased raids throughout Amsterdam, as thousands were dragged from their beds in the middle of the night to be beaten, shot, or thrown into deportation trucks headed for camps within Holland and then to Bergen-Belsen, Auschwitz, or Ravensbrück.

Miep's husband, Henk, also paid daily visits to the Annexe, bringing with him supplies too heavy for Miep to carry. On Saturdays, Henk rode his bicycle to a shop on Rijn Street to borrow books for the hidden people. Each person would make a list of the books wanted, and Henk's return was eagerly awaited.

Three other members of the staff of Travies and Company, Elli Vossen, Victor Kraler, and Jo Koophuis – all of whom knew about the Annexe – visited as often as they could. They did their best to bring cheer to the people whose only hopes for survival lay within their hands.

As the days and nights passed with agonizing slowness, the eight Jews in hiding made every effort to keep themselves occupied. Otto spent many hours each day teaching his daughters. Henk had brought textbooks in maths, history, languages, and literature. As the voice of the BBC brought word of each day's battle results or Allied advances, pins were placed on a map that stretched along the wall of the room everyone shared as a living and eating area. Nights were filled with the sounds of boots tramping over cobbled streets and the whine of sirens as air battles between the Allies and the Germans increased. Sleep came fitfully for the people of the Annexe, and small bags to be carried if escape was necessary, often containing nothing more than a change of underclothes and a few coins, were always close at hand.

Margot grew increasingly quiet and withdrawn. Anne devoted most of her time to her writing, slipping off into a quiet corner to make entries in her diary, or to write little essays or poems marking someone's birthday or anniversary. Anne frequently fought off her fears and loneliness by adding to her collection of movie star pin-ups, the latest of which would be brought by Miep.

The winter of 1942 was marked by harsh winds, freezing temperatures, and increased food shortages. Miep became more concerned about the group she was helping. With fewer and fewer ration stamps to spare, she spent hours each evening and early morning riding her bicycle from shop to shop in search of food for her friends as well as for Henk and herself. When the greengrocer from whom she had bought her vegetables was arrested as a Jewish sympathizer (his wife confessed to Miep that he had sheltered two Jews), she rode many blocks and crossed several canals before discovering a tiny market run by an elderly woman in a basement apartment. Days went by before she could establish enough trust in the old woman to beg for the quantity of food she needed. Then, after a sleepless night, fearful that she might have been followed by the ever-watchful Green Police, Miep returned to find the woman waiting for her with a bag of fresh produce. Miep was grateful for this newest, silent collaborator.

Miep's greatest fear that winter was for the health of her friends in hiding. Fortunately, except for a few minor colds (Anne's was the worst; her muffled coughs under her heavy blanket the concern of all), everyone managed to come through without a severe illness. Two small coal stoves kept everyone reasonably warm and an extra sweater or jacket on the coldest days helped. Ashes from the stoves were smuggled out by Miep or Henk, and garbage was kept to a minimum. Every scrap of food was used somehow, if only to feed Peter Van Daan's cat.

As spring of 1943 burst forth in Amsterdam, some of the worst raids took place. Orphanages protecting Jewish children left behind when their parents were deported were stormed, and the children were seized and carried to waiting trucks bound for the concentration camps. Hospitals and mental institutions were raided, and the victims, often terminally ill, carried in box-cars to unknown destinations.

During that same spring, Miep and Henk found themselves with a new crisis. A friend became desperate for a place in which to hide her son, a university student who had refused to sign an oath of loyalty to the Nazis. After a lengthy conference during which Miep and Henk discussed the problems of feeding and hiding a university student, it was agreed that Karel van der Hart could take refuge with the Gieses.

Summer approached and Miep found it harder and harder to locate enough food for everyone. Often, there was no meat, little butter or milk, and only a small supply of vegetables. Her days were long, and her fears for the safety of those in the Annexe deepened.

For those in the Annexe, new problems were developing. Anne, now thirteen and bursting out of her clothing, was suffering severe headaches and difficulty with her vision. Studying was increasingly painful and her patience was wearing thin. At first, the family considered letting Miep take her to an eye doctor located a short distance away. In the end, however, it was Otto who resolved that, despite Anne's discomfort, no threat to her safety could be risked. Glasses would have to wait.

On several occasions, the Franks and the others in hiding heard bumping noises and other loud disturbances coming from the direction of the warehouses downstairs. Had one of the Travies and Company shippers, one who had not been told of the Annexe, become suspicious of Miep or Henk or the others? And if so, who? Uneasiness and gloom settled over everyone. Now, as Miep and Henk carried the needed supplies up to the Annexe, every effort was taken to avoid further trouble. As they well knew, others in hiding had been betrayed for a few loaves of bread, a little meat, or a new pair of shoes.

The skies over Amsterdam were filled with aircraft that summer. Allied bombing of major German cities were on the increase and Germany had begun to suffer major losses. On the Eastern Front, the Nazis had been defeated at Stalingrad, and the Russians were slowly advancing towards Poland.

The round-ups of Jews continued relentlessly throughout the summer and fall of 1943. Miep and Henk spent many nights listening to the thunder of armoured trucks rolling through the River Quarter of South Amsterdam where they lived. They watched silently the stream of captured Jewish neighbours, surrounded by the Green Police, pass under the windows of their apartment building. Who would be next?

In the winter of 1943, life for the people of the Annexe was more perilous, and for Miep and her band of helpers as well. No one could ignore the black-bordered signs everywhere, threatening execution to those serving in the Dutch Resistance and to anyone caught hiding Jews.

Fears of these reprisals were brought home suddenly to Miep and Henk one evening as they discovered that their young university student, bored by long days spent alone at the apartment, had slipped outside and gone to the racetrack. There, a raid had taken place and Karel was questioned about his address. Foolishly, the boy gave it to his interrogators, and Henk, with great reluctance, had to tell him that he would have to find another place to hide. Henk had other worries about future investigations. He confessed to Miep that for months he had been a member of the Dutch Resistance.

As the months dragged by, several more breakins occurred at the Travies and Company warehouses. After the worst of these, Otto Frank left the safety of his hiding place to phone his partner, Jo Koophuis. Miep and Henk, upon hearing this, rushed to warn Otto and the others, by now badly shaken, not to leave the Annexe again, no matter what might be going on downstairs. More than once, Jews hiding safely for months had been caught by one little careless act, one little slipup in their daily routine.

Anne continued to write in her diary each day. She noted her fears, her secret longings, private jokes, and her growing interest in Peter Van Daan. As the branches of the chestnut tree outside her window took on the first buds of the spring of 1944, she wrote of the rumours of a massive invasion by the Allies.

The Allied invasion did come and the tide began to turn against the Germans. Hopes began to rise among the Jews in the Annexe that the war would soon come to an end and that they would be spared.

On the fifteenth of July, 1944, Anne Frank made her last entry in her diary:

> I can feel the sufferings of millions and yet,
> if I look up into the heavens, I think that

> it will all come right, that this cruelty too
> will end ... that peace and tranquillity
> will return ...

And then, on a warm Friday morning in August of 1944, came the moment everyone had dreaded for two years. As Miep, Elli Vossen, and Jo Koophuis sat working at their desks, a man dressed in civilian clothes suddenly appeared in front of them, brandishing a pistol and ordering them not to move. The three froze at their desks. The man had slipped through the door without making a sound.

Turning from them, the intruder raced down the hall to Victor Kraler's office. Koophuis whispered something to Miep, and Elli began to cry. Koophuis repeated his words, this time begging the two women to leave while they could. Miep refused, determined to stay at her post. But at Koophuis's insistence, Elli ran to the doorway, promising to call Miep's husband and Koophuis's wife from a nearby telephone to warn them of what was happening.

A short time after Elli's departure, Henk came in. Grabbing the Jews' illegal ration cards from her purse, Miep ran to the door, shoving the cards and the money into Henk's hands and motioning to him to leave. In an instant, Henk was gone.

Miep and Jo Koophuis sat glued to their desks. Then, just as silently as the first, a second armed man came through the doorway, ordering Koophuis to follow him as he moved down the hallway and entered Kraler's office. Doors opened and shut again. Then footsteps came down the stairs leading from the Annexe. The Franks and their friends were being taken away.

Miep remained frozen in her chair, too shocked, too stunned to move. Then she heard the sound of familiar voices. Elli and Henk were returning. Saying little to one another, the three left the office and moved down the hallway and on up the stairs to the hiding place. Moving from room to room, they saw overturned furniture, books scattered, and drawers ransacked.

That night, Miep and Henk poked at their meagre supper, eating nothing, saying nothing. Across the table from them sat Karel, who returned to hide with them. Finally, Henk spoke. That afternoon, he had walked to within a block of the offices of Travies and Company. Standing across the street at the canal bridge, he had watched as a dark green van pulled up to number 263 Prinsengracht. As the van came to a stop, two armed men emerged and raced up the steps to the building. Moments later, ten people – eight of them carrying small cloth bags – silently descended the stairs, surrounded by the Green Police. Henk turned his head toward the canal as the sounds of heavy metal doors clanked shut. It was over.

On Friday, 8 May 1945, the Germans surrendered. The empire that was to have lasted for a thousand years had been crushed. During the weeks that

23

followed, Miep and Henk waited anxiously for word of the friends they had protected with their lives for two long years. Then, on June 3, just one month later, the word came. Otto Frank was the sole survivor of the group they had tried so hard to save.

On 4 August 1944, the day of the raid on the Annexe, Victor Kraler and Jo Koophuis, Otto Frank's business partners, had also been arrested. Koophuis was later released because of ill health. Kraler served seven months at a forced labour camp before escaping.

Otto Frank and his family, the Van Daans, and Dr Dussel had been sent to Westerbork concentration camp and were later transferred to Auschwitz, where Mrs Frank died in the infirmary on 6 January 1945; a short time after that Mr Van Daan was gassed. That same winter, Peter Van Daan died while on a death march west of Auschwitz. Anne, Margot, and Mrs Van Daan were taken to Bergen-Belsen where they died of dysentery and typhus some time before the end of March 1945. Anne, the last to die, was not yet sixteen.

Several weeks after Otto's return, Miep Gies reached into her desk and pulled out the little checkered diary she had managed to salvage from the belongings scattered around the Annexe rooms. Handing it to Otto, Miep said, 'Here is your daughter Anne's legacy to you.' One day, Anne's diary would be a legacy shared by the entire world.

During the years following the war, Miep and Henk

slowly picked up the pieces of their shattered lives, finding enough room in their small apartment for Otto Frank, who stayed with them for seven years before moving to Switzerland. In July of 1950, forty-year-old Miep gave birth to a son, Paul.

Each year, on 4 May, along with their countrymen, the Gieses pause to commemorate the Dutch day of mourning, when lights are lit, all transportation ceases, and flowers are placed at the sites where Dutch Resistance fighters were executed. For Miep and Henk, there is another remembrance day, a private one: 4 August, the day of the raid on the Annexe.

2
Oskar and Emilie Schindler

The silent procession of mourners moved slowly through the streets of Jerusalem. Ahead of them was the long, leaden casket of the friend they had come to bury. He was not an Israeli, nor was he a Jew. And yet, he was one of them.

Later, on a little hill overlooking the Valley of Hinnom, the body of Oskar Schindler was buried under a warm November sun. Itzhak was there, and so were Moshe and Juda and Jakob and Helen. They and each of the other *Schindlerjuden* (Schindler Jews) had come to pay final tribute to the Czechoslovakian German who had saved them from the ovens of Auschwitz and Chelmno and Belzev and Treblinka. He had fed them. He had clothed them and given them places to sleep. In the midst of the evil that had once surrounded them, he had offered them *hatikva*, hope.

On 28 April 1908, Oskar Schindler, son of Hans and Louisa and brother of Elfriede Schindler, was born in Zwittau, an industrial city in the mountains of the Moravian Sudetenland, an area in northern Czechoslovakia that had once been a part of Austria.

Oskar had a happy, carefree youth. He went to the local German-speaking grammar school, where he and his fellow students trained for careers in engineering. Like most boys his age, he welcomed the days of summer, when he could indulge his love for fast cars and motorcycles. He raced with the best contenders of the villages and towns of the region, outsmarting many champions as he tore up and down the mountainous land on one of his powerful motorcycles.

During the summer of 1928, Oskar Schindler, now twenty years old, met and married Emilie, a nineteen-year-old girl who was the only child of a prosperous farmer from the nearby village of Alt-Molstein. Relatives and friends of both families were shocked by the brief courtship and hasty wedding ceremony, and none were more incensed than the fathers of the bride and groom.

It was an odd match. Oskar, tall, slim, dashingly handsome, already exhibited the flamboyance, charm, and zest for the fast life so like his father's. Emilie, by contrast, had led a sheltered existence, attending convent schools and dutifully obeying the

27

rules set down by her widowed father and the local parish priest.

Soon after the wedding, Oskar went off to serve the required period of time in the Czechoslovakian Army, while Emilie stayed behind in Zwittau. The military life, with all of its discipline and order, held no appeal, however, and Oskar counted the days until he could resume the life filled with the comforts he had come to love.

Returning to Zwittau a private citizen, Oskar went to work at his father's farm-machinery factory and soon found he was developing great skill in selling and marketing the Schindler products. Rumours began to float about, suggesting that Oskar spent his evenings at the local cafés, drinking and flirting.

In 1935, the Schindler factory closed. Oskar became the regional sales manager for an electrotechnical firm and was away from Emilie for weeks at a time. He amazed his employers with his extraordinary ability to bring in new business. At the same time, because of the nature of his work, Oskar was making valuable contacts with people rising in political and military power throughout the Sudetenland. These contacts would one day play a significant role in Schindler's life.

At a party one evening in 1938, Schindler was introduced to Eberhard Gebauer, an officer of Abwehr, the Secret Intelligence Service of the Wehrmacht, the German Army. Would Oskar be interested, Gebauer asked, in using his skills to gather information for the Third Reich? Assignments would take him across the border into Poland, where the Abwehr wanted to acquire intelligence regarding the strengths and weaknesses of the Polish Army. Schindler jumped at the chance. The excitement of working for such a secret operation held much glamour and appeal for him. Soon, he was commuting between Zwittau and the beautiful city of Kraków, Poland, balancing his work for Gebauer with his expanding interests in the electrotechnical business.

During the month of March, in 1939, Hitler's armies marched into the Sudetenland. By September of that same year, Germany had swept across Poland. Schindler was greatly disturbed, not only by the advances made by Hitler's mighty army, but by the way in which the Jews and Czechs were being treated in the newly occupied territories. Continuing his work with the Abwehr, Schindler became aware of the fact that Gebauer and a number of other officers disapproved of many things that were taking place.

For the next seven months, Oskar Schindler continued to make contacts in southern Poland, dining with leaders in the Polish business and political community as well as with officials representing the German occupation forces. He seemed totally comfortable and in control in both camps, pulling information from the most unlikely sources and flashing his disarming smile across many a dinner table.

During this time, Schindler met Itzhak Stern, who had been a Jewish accountant for a profitable Polish dry goods manufacturer before the German onslaught. Although Stern's responsibilities had been largely taken over by a German supervisor, he was still an employee and an active member of the Jewish business community. Schindler, restless for a new challenge, asked Stern to check into a number of business opportunities he had been investigating for himself. A short time later, Stern presented Schindler with some possibilities. And so Oskar Schindler, now aged thirty-one, with total indifference to the possible consequences, gave up his job as a salesman and bought the little Kraków enamel factory that would become the centre of all of his activities for the next several years.

Schindler's private life had taken on new interests as well. Among these was Ingrid, a beautiful and talented German woman who had recently been named manager of a large Kraków hardware business. (By the autumn of 1939, all businesses owned by Jews in Poland had been taken over by the German occupation.) Ingrid shared Oskar Schindler's enthusiasm for parties, weekends with friends, and socializing with important people. Oskar, who spent little or no time with Emilie in Zwittau, moved into a fashionable apartment on Straszewskiego Street, which had, before the occupation, belonged to a prominent Jewish family.

Schindler continued to rely upon Itzhak Stern for sound business advice regarding his enamel factory, Deutsche Email Fabrik. With his usual energy, he was rapidly expanding the manufacture of enamelware. Soon, through his many contacts with the German occupational forces, he was producing kitchen utensils for the military.

Early one bitterly cold morning in December, Oskar Schindler paid an unannounced visit to Stern, but to Stern's surprise, it was not business the German had in mind. During that visit, Oskar warned Stern that there was soon to be some kind of an action taken against the Jews in the Kazimierz sector of Kraków. Schindler's message was brief. So brief, in fact, that before Stern had time to digest it, Schindler was gone.

Soon after, an *Aktion*, or round-up of Jews – the first of its kind in the city of Kraków – did take place. On street after street and in countless homes throughout the Kazimierz sector, Jews were beaten and robbed. As SS troops rampaged the area, an armoured van carrying six Nazi gunmen acting as mobile killing units raided the five-hundred-year-old Stara Boznica Temple, the oldest synagogue in Poland. As the congregation bent over their prayers, the terrorists stormed down the aisles of the temple and broke open the sacred Ark. Tearing the ancient Torah scroll from the Ark, the Nazis threw the parchment to the floor and demanded that the worshippers spit upon it. Seconds later, guns blasted.

Word of the temple massacre spread quickly throughout the city that night. Many members of the Jewish community who had been sceptical of Schindler's warning now began to fear for their

31

families, their neighbours, and their friends. But Stern also wondered why Oskar Schindler, a German industrialist who was just beginning to make his mark, would risk his reputation for the sake of a few hundred Jews?

Some time during the early spring of 1940, Itzhak Stern paid a visit to Oskar Schindler at his new offices on Lipowa Street. Stern took note of the man. Only the finest of materials for his suits, it appeared. Pure silk shirts and ties, and jewelled rings that sparkled on his long fingers. Nothing but the best for Oskar Schindler. And to complete the picture, that smile – as if the German hadn't a care in the world.

Schindler discussed with Stern his intention of hiring new employees. Stern marvelled at the man. Here he was, after a few short months in Kraków, the head of an expanding company with military contracts and the favour of powerful figures associated with the Wehrmacht's Armaments Inspectorate, and he was asking Itzhak Stern to find him one hundred and fifty Jewish men and women to work in his factory. Was the man insane?

After careful thought, Stern agreed. He would find the workers. That would not be difficult. But there *were* problems. Grave problems.

Among the latest of the German edicts against the Jews were those excluding Jews from the workplace. Jewish professionals as well as blue-collar and factory workers were losing their jobs to non-Jews in massive numbers throughout Poland.

How then, Stern wanted to know, could Schindler

possibly consider the hiring of a *single* Jew – let alone one hundred and fifty – in his factory?

Simple, Schindler replied. His work now involved contracts for the military and would therefore count as essential to the war effort. No one would question Herr Oskar Schindler about his unusual hiring practices. After all, some interesting people had invested heavily in this new and thriving enterprise. People in high places. People with influence.

And so, the first of the Jews were hired. As the months rolled by and production continued to expand, their numbers increased. The hours were long, but the work was steady and the morale of the workers was high. The factory – Deutsche Email Fabrik – had become known as a safe place for Jews. A haven from a world that grew more dangerous with each passing day. Schindler was fair; always kind and courteous. Never too busy to stop and offer a word of encouragement to a weary factory worker.

One day, as Schindler made an inspection of a new department of the factory that would be involved in the production of munitions and shell casings, he received word through one of his many contacts that a new Jewish ghetto was to be established. It would be a walled section, isolated from the rest of Kraków in every respect and guarded by the Kraków police force and the *Judenrat*, a group of Jews appointed by the Nazis as overseers to ensure that the edicts issued by the German command would be obeyed. Now, the Jews were to be isolated from the life they once knew.

A few weeks later, while Schindler made his way

about Kraków, he watched wagons and carts moving slowly through the streets, crammed with whatever possessions a family could gather for the move into the ghetto. Behind the vehicles walked Kraków's Jews, parents carrying infants, children clutching the family kitten, a doll, or a small bag of books. Each day, as Schindler's chauffeur guided his sleek black limousine past a procession, he watched the crowds that lined both sides of the street, taunting the Jews and tossing stones at them. He heard jeering voices rising above the crowd.

Inside the ghetto, a family would be assigned a single room, perhaps two, and a kitchen to be shared by several families. Beyond the tiny window lay a view of the sealed wall with its rows of barbed wire, its gatehouse, and its guards.

Soon after the Nazis had established the Jews in the ghetto, Abraham Bankier, Schindler's office manager, paid a visit to an employment office that had been set up within the ghetto walls to hire men and women for jobs connected with the war production industry. The wages were low and the risks high. Already, there were rumours of Jews who had not returned from a day's work in a Kraków factory.

But Bankier was not concerned with rumours. He knew something about Oskar Schindler that many important people did not know. Schindler was one German you could trust to take care of the Jews who worked for him. He would see to it that they returned home each night. And Oskar Schindler needed more help to work his night shift.

That evening, as Bankier climbed the stairs to his employer's suite of offices at Deutsche Email, he glanced furtively at the trail of women who followed him. How pathetic they looked, fearful and distrusting of the German who said he had work for them. Why? Were there not plenty of non-Jews in Kraków who would jump at the chance to work in such a place? Why Jews?

As the women filed into the spacious office quarters, they could not help but stare at the elegant surroundings. The finest Turkish Oriental rugs were on the floors. On the walls were exquisite paintings and sculptures. The furniture was of elegant woods, upholstered in the most expensive fabrics. Who was this man?

And then they saw him. His smile radiant, his voice reassuring. Oskar Schindler was speaking to them, telling them that they need not worry about themselves. He would see to it that they would be safe. No harm would come to them as long as they were in his employ. Just a few words, and then he was gone.

Oskar Schindler was riding high. Deutsche Email Fabrik was prospering, his influence with the Wehrmacht officers of rank and power continued to expand, and his dealings in black market products had fattened his bank account. When questions arose about the wisdom of employing so many Jews, Schindler just laughed, and steered the conversation onto a discussion of Germany's newest triumphs in the war. Those who might have had the slightest suspicions of the true nature of Schindler's employment practices were rewarded by an expensive gift of some kind.

From time to time, Emilie Schindler would come to Kraków. She loved the city's beauty and enjoyed the chance to leave the provincial atmosphere of Zwittau and the gossip about her husband's long absences. In fact, an appearance by Oskar Schindler was usually marked by an event of importance. The death of a family member; an occasional Easter holiday.

Whenever Emilie Schindler stayed with her husband in Kraków, she would hear news about the worsening conditions in the Jewish ghetto, the unemployment and the hunger, the cruelty of the guards, and the beatings by Polish citizens as well as Nazi overseers. She was troubled by the disappearances of a number of the city's Jews. Rounded up for forced labour at Plaszow, the new concentration camp being built on the outskirts of Kraków, many failed to return at the end of a workday. Emilie Schindler also learned about the sadistic nature of the camp's commandment, Amon Goeth.

Oskar Schindler's practice of employing Jews at Deutsche Email brought comfort to his wife. She was proud of her husband's work, although she was aware of the risks involved. Twice he had been arrested by suspicious authorities at SS headquarters. Only through his cleverness and the effects of some heavy bribes, was he able to secure his release. Touring her husband's plant on her visits, Mrs Schindler met many of the men and women who worked in the munitions department. They were well-treated, and deeply loyal to the man who had given them some hope of a better existence. Mrs Schindler also knew the strange circumstances of their employment. Instead of paying wages to his Jewish workers, Schindler handed rations of food and supplies to them and turned over to the local SS headquarters a daily fee for every person who worked for him!

In the months that followed one of Emilie Schindler's visits, conditions at Kraków deteriorated. There were new executions and disappearances, and hangings in the public square for those who tried to hide their Jewish friends. One morning, more than one thousand men from the ghetto were marched to the cattle trains and deported to unknown destinations.

Schindler learned from reliable contacts of still another *Aktion* at the ghetto. Upon hearing the news, he quickly set up as many cots as could be crowded within the walls of Deutsche Email. If the worst came, at least he would be able to shelter those people who were working at the factory.

On a morning in June 1942, the terror began. Roused from their beds, men, women, and children of the Kraków ghetto were forced from their rooms and herded onto the streets. Pushed, shoved, and beaten by SS guards and Gestapo police, the men were separated from the women, and the women from their children. Those who protested were gunned down.

The Jews watched as their rooms were raided, beds set afire, and the elderly and the sick tossed from open windows. The *Aktion* raged throughout the day, and then the shootings began. Gunfire blasted into the crowds of innocent victims huddled together in the heat of the warm summer day.

Seven thousand Jews were murdered that day, or deported to death camps. This was just the beginning of the many raids that followed, not only at Kraków, but at Warsaw, Lodz, and all of the other Eastern European ghettos as the Nazis moved toward the Final Solution – Adolf Hitler's master plan for the total extermination of the Jewish population. It was on this day that Oskar Schindler made his ultimate commitment to the five hundred and fifty Jews who were now in his employ. He would protect them, somehow. He would find a way to save them from the final horror.

Later, some would say of Oskar Schindler that he was foolish to take the risks that he took. After a third arrest, many of those closest to him warned him that one day his luck would run out. To these unheeded protests, he would merely shrug and laugh. On more than one occasion, Schindler spent large sums of money in bribes to a local official, an officer of the SS, or a ranking member of the Armaments Inspectorate. Each time he was confronted by a new challenge, a new threat to the safety of his workers or to himself, he would emerge unscathed, undaunted by the dangers that faced him. His energies and his resourcefulness knew no bounds, and the Jews who worked for him marvelled at the man.

On March 13, 1943, the war industry facilities at the Plaszow labour camp outside of Kraków were completed and the Kraków ghetto was closed. On Lieutenant Amon Goeth's orders, all of the ghetto's elderly and terminally ill Jews were loaded onto cattle cars bound for the death camps. The Jews who were left, including all of Schindler's workers, were to be sent to the camp and put to work in each of several factories that were to go into operation. Schindler protested that *his* plant was also engaged in essential war industry. Had not Deutsche Email received the highest of praise from the head of the German Occupational Command? Besides, there were any number of things Amon Goeth could avail himself of through Schindler's connections with the black market.

Amon Goeth was a greedy man with insatiable needs. Perhaps Schindler could help with the furnishing of Amon's new villa at the Plaszow camp.

After a talk that lasted into the early hours of the morning, a deal was struck between the two: The Jews in Schindler's factory would be interned at the Plaszow camp, but continue to work for Deutsche Email, marching each day under heavy guard from the camp to the factory and back again in two shifts covering the twenty-four-hour workday.

As the weeks passed, however, Schindler noted changes in his workers. Increasingly gaunt and fearful, their eyes and vacant expressions seemed to hide secrets they dared not reveal. Frequently late or absent from their work stations, the workers would tell Schindler they had been ordered into one of the labour gangs operating within the camp. Soon, there were stories of floggings and public hangings, which the prisoners were forced to witness. Schindler also learned of one of Amon Goeth's favourite pastimes – standing on his villa balcony before breakfast in the morning and firing several shots into a group of Jews marching by.

Enraged, Schindler demanded that his workers be released from the Plaszow camp. He would provide quarters for them near the Deutsche Email factory. After the customary bribes and promises, Amon Goeth agreed to let Oskar keep his workers – at extraordinary cost to Schindler. What mattered most in the world to Schindler now was the protection of the Jews. They would be housed in clean quarters, given food twice a day, and treated like human beings. There would be no beatings, no dying from starvation or overwork.

Other Polish Jews were not so fortunate. Week by week, trainloads of prisoners were brought into the Plaszow camp, the numbers grew to more than thirty-five thousand. Starvation and disease were rampant among the prisoners. And in the presence of all of this evil, Amon Goeth was amassing a fortune in juggled account books and bribes.

Late in the summer of 1944, as the Germans took heavy losses along the Eastern Front and the Russians began their advance into Poland, Schindler found out that the Plaszow camp was to be disbanded and its prisoners were to be 'relocated,' the men to Gross-Rosen and the women to Auschwitz. Certain that the Plaszow Jews were marked for extermination, Schindler began to formulate a plan. An impossible plan, perhaps, but one worth pursuing. Because to Oskar Schindler, nothing was impossible.

Timing was everything. There was but one thing to do: Move Deutsche Email Fabrik to a safer place.

Leaving the factory in trusted hands, Schindler drove across the border and south, toward the rolling terrain of the Jessenik Mountains he had once known and loved so much. Through his contact, he discovered a textile plant that was located on the outskirts of Brünnlitz, near the city of Zwittau. Attached to the plant was an unused annexe, which proved to be exactly what Schindler was looking for. Workshops would be set up on the first floor, along with a small apartment for himself. On the second floor, there was adequate room for barracks.

After extensive appeals to Schindler's influential sources in Berlin, permission for the move was granted. Hurrying back to Poland, a list of prisoners began forming in his mind. Of utmost importance were his own workers. They would be the first to move, but there were others. On his many visits to Amon Goeth's villa at the Plaszow camp, there were scores of prisoners with whom he had come in contact. Among these were people who worked in the uniform factory. He could use them at the new plant. Schindler's list was growing.

After almost two months, the Brünnlitz factory

camp was ready for production. Male prisoners were to be moved first and the women to follow. The train journey would take several days to complete, but the workers were not fearful. Schindler was in charge. They would be safe. All would be well.

But all was not well. Following the arrival of the men at the Brünnlitz camp, months went by with no sign of the three hundred women Schindler had included in his list. The men, many of whom had wives in the group, became frantic. What had gone wrong?

At last, Schindler learned the truth. The Deutsche Email women had been deported to Auschwitz, the death camp near Birkenau.

Schindler tried everything to acquire the release of the women, but the usual bribes would not do. One day, as he contemplated his next move with his old friend Itzhak Stern (who had been on Schindler's list), a secretary came into his office. Studying the young woman for a moment, Schindler had an idea. Pointing to a large diamond ring on one of his fingers, Schindler offered it to the woman, in return for a favour. Without hesitation, she agreed to help.

Following Schindler's orders, the woman filled a large suitcase with the finest foods and drink she could carry. Then, clutching a list of the names of the three hundred women, she started off for Auschwitz.

Days passed, with no word from the woman. Emilie Schindler, who had joined her husband once again, grew extremely anxious, having known the woman's family for many years.

Then, one icy winter morning soon after the secretary's return to Brünnlitz, a train arrived. As the huge doors were opened, the women stumbled out. Full of lice, racked by dysentery and typhus, and in rags, the women stared at the sight before them. Standing before an open gate and surrounded by SS guards, stood Oskar Schindler in a Tyrolean hat and fur-trimmed coat. Many years later, one of the women said of him, 'He was our father, he was our mother, he was our only faith. He never let us down.'

From the autumn of 1944 until 7 May 1945, Schindler's factory continued to operate. The women slowly recovered from their Auschwitz ordeal (the only such group to have been released from the camp during the entire war), due partly to Emilie Schindler's remarkable care. To them, she was a saint, nursing them with medicines she got, at great risk, from the black market. At any time of the day, she could be seen carrying portions of thick, steaming soup to the infirmary where a number of Jewish physicians worked.

In a memoir published in 1974, Schindler wrote of his wife's loyalty. 'My wife, Emilie, shared my views on the importance of saving Jewish lives . . . she often worked a fourteen- to sixteen-hour day alongside me, as we faced one crisis after another.'

Throughout the seven months that Brünnlitz

was in operation, there were indeed many crises. Schindler was arrested for the third time, before his wife finally arranged for his release. There were food shortages requiring many black market dealings with local merchants, and frequent scuffles with some of the more zealous of the SS guards posted at the camp. And there were the two deportation trains that pulled up in the rail yard outside of the camp, full of half-starved prisoners bound for nowhere. Upon hearing that the guards in charge of the trains intended to shoot everyone inside who was still alive, the Schindlers demanded the release of the prisoners and took them in.

During the first few days of May 1945, with the end of the war just days away, the SS guards assigned to Brünnlitz deserted the camp. When the Russians arrived on 7 May, one of the Jews slipped a letter to the officer in charge. In it was a testimonial attesting to the Schindlers' courage and determination in saving the lives of the Jews.

A short time later, the Russians allowed the Schindlers to leave Brünnlitz. Accompanied by about ten Jews, they journeyed through Allied lines, stopping at roadblocks to present their letter to the authorities, sometimes Russian, and at other times Czech. One morning after stopping at a local inn to rest, the little group discovered their car broken into – and all of their food and clothing gone. Jewels and money that they had hoped to use in their escape had been ripped out of a secret pocket in one of the car doors. Later, after a long journey in box-cars and on foot, the Schindlers and their former prisoners arrived in the American zone. Hungry and sick with exhaustion, they met a Jewish officer who made arrangements for their departure to South America.

After the war, Oskar and Emilie Schindler, with the help of some of their devoted Jewish workers, bought a small farm in Argentina's Buenos Aires province, where they remained for almost ten years. But farming was not for Oskar Schindler, and in 1957 the Schindlers went bankrupt. Supported by the Jewish organization B'nai B'rith, he tried a number of commercial ventures, none of which was successful. He returned to Germany, moving into a small apartment in Frankfurt, again with funds supplied by many of his former workers, while Emilie Schindler remained in Buenos Aires, where she continued to live for many years.

In 1961, a number of the Jews who had worked for Schindler and who had moved to Israel, among them Itzhak Stern, invited Schindler to Jerusalem to be honoured by Yad Vashem, the Holocaust Memorial Museum, as one of the Righteous Among Nations. This is a distinction given to the men and women who had risked their lives to rescue Jews from Hitler's tyranny.

What motivated Oskar Schindler to help the Jews? He was not a religious man, nor was he a man of the highest ethical standards. To those who knew him best, there was no easy explanation for his actions.

Oskar Schindler's remaining years were difficult

ones. Appearing on the streets of Frankfurt, he was frequently hissed and taunted by those who knew of his activities during the war. Many Germans continued to be fiercely anti-Semitic, and their attitudes took a desperate toll on the man who had once fought so tirelessly for the lives of his workers. With a small pension that was finally awarded him by the German government, Schindler divided his time between Frankfurt and Jerusalem. On one of his visits, he expressed his desire to be buried on the hills above the city, the only place on earth where he thought he could find peace.

On a warm November day in 1974, the Catholic priest at a cemetery on the hill overlooking the Valley of Hinnom in the ancient city of Jerusalem intoned his final prayers. Oskar Schindler, German industrialist, spy, entrepreneur, and rescuer of more than twelve hundred Jews, found his peace at last.

After the service, those who had come to mourn him inched closer to his grave and stood in silence, each remembering the years that had gone before. As the sun rose higher in the sky, someone began to sing softly. It was, perhaps, a final tribute to the man who, in the midst of unsurpassed evil, had brought them hope.

3
Defiance in Denmark

Early one April morning in 1940, the skies over Denmark were filled with German aircraft. Swooping down close to the ground, the planes dumped thousands of green leaflets. The people were to remain calm, the messages read. There was nothing to fear from the Germans of the Third Reich. But within hours, Denmark was swarming with tanks, SS troops, and Gestapo police, who quickly defeated the Danish army. Without warning, Denmark had been invaded and conquered.

The Germans went to work immediately, making noisy speeches in public gathering places and handing out anti-Semitic literature encouraging the isolation of Jews from Danish society. But the campaign against the Jews backfired. The Germans had counted on the kind of cooperation they had had in their own country and in Eastern Europe. Denmark was different. Its Jewish population of roughly eight thousand had been totally integrated since the early part of the nineteenth century. Danes were Danes, whether they were Jews, Catholics, Protestants, or otherwise.

During the 1930s, Christian X, King of Denmark, had warned the German ambassador to Denmark that anti-Semitism was unacceptable. And as news about the violent raids against the Jews in Germany spread, the Danes were angry and ashamed. In ceremonies marking the one hundredth anniversary of the great Crystal Synagogue in Copenhagen, the king defied the actions and participated in the services, accompanied by his entire family.

This mistake on the part of the Germans combined with another unusual situation. The Danes were considered by the Nazis to be purely Aryan like themselves. So when the people of Denmark openly defended the Jews, the Germans changed their tactics. Until 1943, no Jewish businesses were shut down, university professors and other people of influence continued their work, and synagogues stayed open. Then came the new orders from the German high command.

In 1943, the Danish government was ordered to begin legislation against the Jews, ghettos were to be established, and the yellow Star of David was to be worn by every Jew.

The Danes took to the streets in protest, and

bishops and clergy throughout the country took to their pulpits. King Christian offered to move into a ghetto, declaring that it would be an honour to wear the Jewish star.

Tensions mounted. When scores of Danish army officers were arrested, the navy sank its own entire fleet. The Danish Resistance, which for some time had been helping Jews leave the country, began sabotaging German bases, stealing weapons, and instigating riots and strikes in major cities. On 29 August 1943, the Danish government resigned and the Nazis took control, finalizing plans for the deportation of Denmark's Jews to the death camps.

The Germans secretly set 1 October, the beginning of the Jewish New Year, as the date for the round-ups, knowing that the Jews would be easy targets as they gathered in homes and synagogues for the holy days.

And then some unexpected events took place. Helmut von Moltke, a German count, found out about the plan through his underground spy network and got word to the Danish Resistance. (He was later executed.) At the same time, a German shipping magnate in Copenhagen named Georg von Duckwitz received a top-secret letter from Berlin ordering him to prepare four of his largest ships for the deportation of Denmark's Jews. At enormous personal risk, the businessman passed the information on to the Swedish ambassador and two members of the former Danish government.

By sundown on the evening before Rosh

Hashanah, warnings of the scheduled round-ups spread to the Danes, who went to their Jewish friends to offer their homes as shelter until a means of escape could be found.

That same night, while Danes were literally pulling their Jewish neighbours off the streets, a small group of Resistance fighters met at the home of the Bishop of Copenhagen to agree upon plans for a daring rescue operation. Under cover of darkness, the Jews would be taken across the sea to Sweden, a neutral country that had offered to give safe haven to war refugees. Transportation would be by private vessels – motorboats, yachts, fishing boats, and even rowboats would be used.

The Danes went into action. For the next three months, one of the war's most extraordinary sea rescues took place. Night after night, thousands of tiny vessels stole past enemy warships. When the mission was finally completed, eight thousand Jews had been saved.

Throughout that time, citizens of all ages in Denmark showed remarkable courage. Once, a group of young students broke into Copenhagen's Crystal Synagogue and removed one hundred Torah scrolls, prayer books, and other precious treasures, storing them in the cellars of Protestant churches throughout the city. Another time, the minister of a remote village church hid one of the country's leading rabbis, along with his entire family. Peter Freuchen, the famous explorer, was arrested twice for rescuing Jews. He escaped both times, despite the fact that the Germans had removed his wooden leg to keep him from running away.

Jørgen Kieler, his brother, and his two sisters were college students, sharing a small apartment in the city of Copenhagen. As members of the Resistance, their quarters were a meeting place for other students and cadets involved in the rescue missions. Their apartment housed an important underground printing office and a hoard of weapons stolen from the Nazis.

Making contact with some fishermen and the crew of a small boat that ferried supplies to a lighthouse between Denmark and Sweden, Jørgen and his sisters mapped out two evacuation routes leading from the city. Then, two of the students stationed themselves at a hiding place on the shoreline, where they sheltered escaping Jews until a rescue boat arrived. Fifteen hundred Jews were eventually saved.

One member of Kieler's team didn't live to see the end of the war. Cato Bakmann, a medical student who operated the printing presses, was discovered as he worked in the apartment of a surgeon at the Bispebberg Hospital. Shot while trying to escape through an open window, the young man died a few hours later as an emergency room nurse held him in her arms. He and the nurse had married less than a month before.

The Danish people continued their support and compassion for the Jews after the Germans were defeated. As the refugees returned, each was given 4,050 kroner by the Danish government. Homes that had not been destroyed by the Nazis were given back to their Jewish owners. Many Jews found that their lawns and gardens had been carefully tended and their refrigerators were filled with food. A Jewish girl who had been one of several hundred captured by the Germans was met by her neighbours, given flowers, and presented with the keys to her apartment. Inside, on her kitchen table, was an envelope containing a large sum of money collected by people in the neighbourhood. Near the envelope was a note:

This is for your initial expenses.

4
The Secrets of Le Chambon

André and Magda Trocmé first came to Le Chambon-sur-Lignon in 1935, when André accepted a post as pastor of the Protestant temple. (A Protestant church in France is called a temple.) They were pacifists, opposed to violence. The people of Le Chambon took an immediate liking to the Trocmés, and soon the temple was the spiritual centre of this remote peasant village high in the mountains of southern France. Year by year, as news of Germany's treatment of the Jews spread, André's sermons on nonviolence took on new meaning.

In 1938, the young minister started a secondary school based on his theories and practices. One of his first teachers was Édouard Theis, a classmate from the University of Paris. Like André, Édouard was a conscientious objector, opposed to war. Édouard Theis became André's right arm, serving as director of the school and as an assistant minister at the temple.

Word of the new school quickly spread to Central and Eastern Europe, and young Jewish refugees began arriving in the village. New teachers were added to the faculty, among them André's wife, Magda, and Édouard Theis's wife, Mildred. Since there was no money for a school building, classes were held in homes and boardinghouses, and in the temple annexe.

When France fell to the Germans in the summer of 1940, the country was divided into two zones. Le Chambon became a part of the southern zone, which was known as Vichy France. For a time, the Vichy government under Marshal Pétain left the southern towns and villages to themselves, with an occasional inspection or restriction ordered to pacify the Germans.

But it was not long before news of Nazi round-ups and deportations of Jews in northern France reached Le Chambon, and the people lived in guarded calm, concerned for the Jewish students and for other refugees who had begun to arrive in the village.

Once, when a new order demanded that the flag of Vichy France be flown above the temple annexe, the teachers refused. And when André was told to ring the temple bell in honour of Pétain's birthday, the bell stayed silent. One day the government's minister of youth arrived at the school to enlist recruits for his newly established Youth Corps, a Nazi propaganda organization. The students responded by handing the minister a letter protesting the deportation of 28,000 Jews from Paris. Several days later, André received his first threat from Vichy officers in charge of the region. All Jews living in the village would be required to register at regional headquarters.

During the days that followed, André and his people developed a plan to protect the Jewish refugees. Every home and farm in the area was put on alert and word was passed that, at a given signal, the Jews were to escape into the dense woods of the surrounding countryside.

Late one night, two weeks after André had received his threat, a convoy of Vichy police followed by official cars and buses moved through the darkened streets of the village. All was quiet. Word had travelled quickly.

André was summoned to the village square and questioned by the Vichy chief of police, whose department had learned that a number of Jews were living in the village. The minister was threatened with deportation and ordered to hand over a list of Jewish names. The police would remain in the village overnight, the chief continued. In the morning the buses would take the Jews to Vichy headquarters.

When the minister was finally released, he walked through the blacked-out streets to his home and gave the signal for the evacuation. One by one, village boy scouts and Bible class leaders spread their warnings to the Jews. All night long, as the police waited to fill their buses, people crept silently through the darkness.

On the following morning, Édouard Theis and André Trocmé preached to a capacity crowd that filled every seat and jammed the pavement leading to the temple entrance. Speaking of the Bible's teachings about the 'cities of refuge' that God had chosen as hiding places to people in need of protection, the ministers urged their people to provide such a refuge for the Jews of Le Chambon.

While André and his people were gathered in the temple, they were unaware that the military police had interrupted an emergency meeting of the mayor's council and had ordered that the Jews be rounded up for a census-taking.

Throughout the afternoon, the police waited for the arrival of the Jews; when none appeared, they began searching every house and public building in the area, but they found no one. The next day, the search spread to the surrounding countryside, where a Jewish woman and her son were discovered and arrested. The son was later released, but the woman never returned.

During the long months that followed, a number of Vichy police became involved in Le Chambon's rescue operation. Phones would ring in the middle of the night, and cryptic messages would warn the listener of a planned raid. Trocmé's 'city of refuge' was gaining support.

One night during the bitter winter of 1941, Magda Trocmé heard a knock on the door. Opening it, she faced a woman covered with snow. She was a refugee, she said. A German Jew who had crossed the northern border and fled south to Vichy France. Someone along the way had told her what was happening in Le Chambon. Magda urged the woman in and sat her in a chair by the fire. Later, she provided the woman with food and a warm bed.

That same winter, André travelled to Marseilles to meet with Burns Chalmers, an American Quaker active in getting Jewish children released from French concentration camps. Chalmers had also heard of Le Chambon's rescue operations. Could Trocmé and his people find refuge for these children? Soon, an old steam train appeared at the little station that served the villages of Le Chambon and Le Mazet. In it were the first children from the camps.

In November of 1942, southern France was overrun by the Germans. Marshal Pétain's government was reduced to a puppet show. The entire country was now under Nazi control.

In the months that followed, the people of Le Chambon and their growing number of refugees suffered many hardships. There was little food and many were hungry. Week by week, the steam train arrived with the newest refugees. During the summer of 1943, sixty Jews were housed in the Trocmé home at one time or another. André, Édouard, and Roger Darcissac (the head of Le Chambon's state school) worked to find other hiding places for people and helped many to escape across the border into Switzerland.

On 13 February 1943, as Magda Trocmé was

preparing dinner, she heard the familiar knock on the door. Major Silvani, the new chief of police for the surrounding region, and one of his lieutenants came to the Trocmé home and demanded to see André. He was to be arrested.

Magda ran to the basement and warned several of the refugees to get into their hiding places. Returning to the officers and André, she announced that the evening meal was ready. Sit down and eat, she ordered everyone – including the two police officers.

That night, André Trocmé, Édouard Theis, and Roger Darcissac were taken to an internment camp where prisoners were held before being sent to the death camps. Within days of their arrival, the three started a discussion group with a few of the prisoners. At first the men came reluctantly, sitting silently on the narrow cots lining André's prison barracks. Most of the men were leaders of the French underground.

Before long, more and more men came, and André asked the guards for a larger room to hold the meetings. The authorities became concerned. Several of the guards began attending the sessions, always sitting in the back of the room. After a month at the camp, Trocmé and his two friends were suddenly freed. Within days of their release, the camp was liquidated and its prisoners sent to the death camps.

Rescue efforts in Le Chambon continued until the end of the war. They were not without their tragedies. Daniel Trocmé, a cousin of André's, died in the Maidanek death camp in Poland on 4 April 1944. Jean-Pierre Trocmé, the eldest of the Trocmé children, died weeks before the Allied liberation.

Many years after the war, André and Magda Trocmé attended an international conference on nonviolence in Munich, Germany. While there, they met Julius Schmahling, a German retired professor who had once been an army major in charge of the region surrounding Le Chambon.

André and Magda asked Herr Schmahling why it was that Le Chambon had not been annihilated, even though it was known to be a haven for Jewish refugees. The Gestapo had raided Daniel Trocmé's dormitory at the school and André and Édouard themselves had been forced into hiding.

Herr Schmahling's reply was brief. He had been raised in the Catholic Church. He had followed some orders and he had ignored others. What had touched him was the quiet resistance of the peasants of Le Chambon. That, he answered, was something the Germans could never destroy.

5
Padre Niccacci's Assisi Underground

At dawn on the morning of 19 October 1943, a small cluster of men – eleven in all – hurried silently past balconied rows of pink stone houses in the medieval Italian hilltown of Assisi. Making their way along the maze of narrow alleyways, the men arrived at the train station just in time for the 6.00 a.m. express to Florence. Led by a monk dressed in his clerical habit, the group boarded the nearest car and rushed towards the first empty compartment, opened a door, and disappeared inside.

For a time, the men continued their silence as the train moved through the rolling countryside, past olive groves and grazing cattle. It was all beautiful and peaceful; far removed from the horror they had experienced only a few hours before.

Finally, one of the men, Padre Rufino Niccacci, spoke. Reaching into his robes, he brought out ten small prayer books, and handed one to each passenger. In case of trouble, he warned them. Who would interrupt a man absorbed in his daily prayers?

The men had reason to be cautious and fearful. One careless gesture or reference to their true identities could cost them their lives. Ten of these men were running away. Their only hope for survival rested on the shoulders of this thirty-two-year-old monk, a peasant of the hill country. A stranger.

In 1943, Italy was in a state of turmoil. Mussolini, Italy's fascist dictator and Hitler's ally, was in prison. By summer's end, Italy had signed an armistice with the Allies, and thousands of Italian soldiers had deserted the army. In retaliation, the Germans had marched into Rome. On 18 October, less than a month later, over one thousand Jewish men, women, and children had been deported to Auschwitz. The raids had begun.

The ten Jewish refugees speeding to Florence with Padre Niccacci that morning had escaped the round-up, fleeing with nothing but the clothing on their backs. They had lost everything – their wives, their children, their relatives, and their homes.

As the men sat clutching their books and practising their prayers, the train slowed down. They were approaching Perugia, the padre whispered. They were to be alert, stay as calm as possible and, above all, to keep their eyes focused on the pages before them. Then the whistle blew and the train screeched to a stop.

Padre Niccacci, his eyes fixed on the compartment's window, watched as a small scattering of passengers left the train and a much larger number of people raced across the platform to board. Everywhere he looked, Gestapo troops kept guard, their glances darting from one passenger to the next, searching.

Suddenly, the door to the compartment flew open. A Gestapo officer walked in with his Italian interpreter, demanding to see papers. Quickly, Padre Niccacci handed over the letter from his *monsignore*, Bishop Giuseppe Placido Nicolini, identifying the ten Jews as Christians returning home to Florence after a holy pilgrimage to Assisi.

The officer turned his attention to an elderly, bearded Jew sitting in the corner seat, demanding to see his identification papers. The old man, a rabbi dressed in monk's robes, went through the motions of looking for the nonexistent papers when suddenly an air raid siren sounded. Seconds later, planes roared overhead and there was the blast of an explosion.

The officer ran from the compartment and out of the train to seek shelter, followed by swarms of German soldiers scrambling for cover. The train started to move, pulling out of the station with agonizing slowness. While the engine built up steam, bombs ripped through the roof of the stationhouse. The British were attacking the German airfield outside of Perugia, and some of their firepower had missed its mark.

While Padre Niccacci and his 'pilgrims' watched the planes of the Royal Air Force fly off into the distance, the train to Florence gradually picked up speed and completed its journey. Upon their arrival, the ten Jewish refugees were placed under the care of Cardinal Elio della Costa, Archbishop of Florence, while plans were made for an escape route to Genoa, and then north to Switzerland. So ended the Assisi underground's first rescue operation. In the tense year ahead, hundreds more would follow.

During the weeks that followed Padre Niccacci's return from the city of Florence, the Germans tightened their hold on Italy. Driving north from Rome, they soon had control of the country, and military convoys bearing swastikas became a common sight along the highways leading to the front lines. But for the moment, no German soldiers patrolled the streets of Assisi, whose Fascist mayor, Arnaldo Fortini, assured his people that their holy shrines would be spared.

For a time, life went on as usual in the village, the bells of the basilica and the other monasteries and convents alternating with the rumble of enemy tanks lumbering along in the distance. But an uneasy calm pervaded, a feeling that something was about to happen.

One afternoon, Padre Niccacci sat in the little piazza outside the Cafe Minerva finishing his Wednesday game of draughts with Luigi Brizi, the printer. Looking up from the table, he saw Emilia Cargol, Bishop Nicolini's niece, hurrying towards him. The *monsignore* wished to see him immediately, she said.

Leaving his unfinished game of draughts, the padre followed Emilia through the narrow streets and alleyways that led to the bishop's palace. When Bishop Nicolini received him, something in his manner alerted the padre that this was no ordinary summons. Nodding in the direction of two other priests in the room, the *monsignore* proceeded to explain the reason for the meeting.

There had been another terrible raid. This time in the northern city of Trieste. A young Italian Jew, Giorgio Kropf, one of twenty who had escaped, had appeared at the basilica that morning begging for somewhere for them to hide. Would the padre take charge of the situation?

Where would Niccacci find shelter for twenty Jews in Assisi? Most of the people in this little hilltown had never even seen a Jew, much less hidden one.

The bishop continued. There was the matter of preparing false papers for the Jews. The Germans were checking all travellers for identity cards now. False IDs would have to be prepared for everyone. The bishop announced that he was appointing Padre Niccacci chairman of Assisi's committee to aid Jews.

Late that night, a silent assemblage of exhausted Jewish refugees trudged up the steep steps leading to the Cloister of the Sisters of Saint Clare, who had agreed to house the refugees in their hostel. At the gate stood Padre Niccacci, welcoming each person who passed through.

Once inside, the people were taken to their rooms, while Giorgio Kropf waited at a reception desk in the darkened hallway. Next to him, the padre went over details of his plan with Sister Amata, one of the few nuns permitted to speak with anyone from outside the convent.

Then came the request Padre Niccacci had dreaded. Sister Amata was asking Giorgio to collect the Jews' identity cards. There were none, the padre announced.

But this was the law, Sister Amata argued. The police would be checking the guest book for names and identification papers. The mother abbess would have to be consulted.

Holding his ground, Padre Niccacci demanded to speak with Mother Giuseppina, the cloister abbess. A few minutes later, the priest was peering through a tiny, double-grilled window. On the other side sat the mother abbess. This was her closest contact with the outside world. For the second time, Padre Niccacci explained the presence of the refugees and the reason for their lack of ID papers.

Mother Giuseppina listened attentively, her hands tightly clasped. At last she spoke, giving her word that the Jews would be protected at all costs. The abbess promised that the nuns would take a vow of secrecy, revealing nothing of the whereabouts of the twenty refugees. The Jews would be housed and properly fed and attended to for as long as their stay at the cloister was required.

The abbess had but one request. Would the padre

65

explain it all to the sisters? Except for those who served the reception hall and the guest rooms, the Clares were monastic, having had no contact with worldly events since the moment they took their vows. Would Niccacci explain to them about the Nazis and the Germans and the Jews?

A short time later, Padre Niccacci addressed the sisters as they gathered in the convent chapel. He told the nuns about the Nazis, reminding them that God had commanded Saint Francis give comfort and shelter to the outcast lepers of his day. He suggested that here was a divine opportunity to embrace the persecuted victims of the present-day world. By coming to the aid of twenty Jewish refugees, they would be following in the steps of the saint himself.

As the vesper bells rang softly in the chapel tower, the Cloister of the Sisters of Saint Clare, shaken by the news they had just heard, solemnly took their vows of secrecy and silence.

On a Sunday, as Bishop Nicolini conducted mass at the Basilica of Saint Francis, there was a rustling at the back of the church. Glancing in the direction of the commotion, he and the other priests at the altar were shocked by what they saw. There, at the entrance, stood a German officer. As everyone in the basilica sat in stunned silence, the officer presented his demands. Arnaldo Fortini, the mayor of Assisi, and Bishop Nicolini were to report to Captain Stolmann at headquarters.

Who was Captain Stolmann? Mayor Fortini asked the officer. And where was headquarters?

Across the piazza, the officer answered. At the Hotel Subasio.

From his stance at the altar, the bishop spotted Padre Nicacci and directed him to accompany the mayor to the hotel. Then, he defiantly stepped to the pulpit and addressed his congregation.

As the padre and Fortini moved outside, they struggled to take in what they saw. Just yards away was a German panzer tank, its gun aimed at the sacred basilica.

Minutes later, the two were ushered into the old hotel, its lobby swarming with German officers. The peaceful hilltown of Assisi had, within one brief hour, been overtaken without the firing of a single shot.

Ordering the two men to follow him, the lieutenant proceeded to the room that had been designated as the headquarters for Stadtkommissar Hauptmann Ernst Stolmann, commandant of the town of Assisi.

Stolmann described the German takeover and delivered his ultimatum: Under penalty of death, the people of Assisi would relinquish all arms within twenty-four hours, a night curfew would be in effect from dusk to dawn, and any act of sabotage or interference with the military would result in execution.

Then, the final order was announced: twelve citizens were to be brought to headquarters the following morning as hostages. In the event of any unpleasant encounter or attack upon the military presence, three hostages would be executed for each German life that was lost.

Hostages? Delivered by the mayor of the sacred

town of Assisi, a man decorated by the great Mussolini himself, a loyal Fascist who had marched on Rome during the 1922 takeover and had ruled Assisi for twenty-one years?

The three men eyed one another silently. Finally, the commandant spoke. By the way, were there any Jews living in Assisi? And if so, how many?

The twenty Jews who had gone into hiding at the Cloister of the Sisters of Saint Clare had come from all over Europe.

There was Edward Gelb and his wife, Mathilde, and their three daughters, Deborah, Hella, and Hanna. They were Yugoslavs who had fled to Trieste when the Nazis had overrun their country. Gelb's father had grown up in Poland and later sought a better life in Belgrade, Yugoslavia. Giulio Kropf and his wife were Viennese, Paolo Jozsa was Hungarian, and the rest, including Rita and Otto Maionica, were northern Italians.

They were a mixed group, ranging in age from very young to very old. They came from many different backgrounds and interests: one was a physician, another a rabbi, and still another a young artist. But they all shared a common enemy, Nazi Germany.

And now that enemy was in Assisi, its soldiers patrolling every corner, every piazza, every alleyway, its tanks and guns aimed at the holiest of shrines. How safe were they in the cloister? How long could the sisters, the padre, and the bishop hold out against such powerful forces?

*

The house in Amsterdam, Netherlands, where Anne Frank and her family hid from the Nazis.

Dit is een foto, zoals
ik me zou wensen,
altijd zo te zijn.
Dan had ik nog wel
een kans om naar
Holywood te komen.
Annefrank.
10 Oct. 1942

A photograph of Anne Frank. The handwritten caption reads:
This is a photo as I would wish myself to look all the time.
Then I would maybe have a chance to come to Hollywood.
Anne Frank, 10 Oct. 1942

A photograph of Miep Gies,
the woman who hid Anne
Frank and her family,
probably taken in 1987.

The S.S. Bodyguard marching past Hitler in January, 1937.

Oskar Schindler.

Jews being rounded up in Poland.

The Star of David, which Jews were forced to wear.

André and Magda Trocmé with their children. From left to right: Daniel, Jacques, Jean-Pierre, and Nelly, around 1935.

A desecrated Torah scroll, 1938.

Padre Rufino Niccacci being honored in 1974.

Willy Minke.

Mrs. Willy Minke.

On the morning after the German commandant issued his demands, Mayor Fortini handed in his resignation. Infuriated, the Germans carried out their first raid.

As fresh troops arrived from Perugia, Foligno, another Italian bases, SS and Gestapo units surrounded the town of Assisi. They set up roadblocks and spread out to all parts of the town, searching for Jews.

Soon, there was the shouting of orders, the clash of boots on stairways and steps, the banging of rifle butts on doors and windows. Hearing the clamour and realizing what was happening, Padre Niccacci raced to the cloister, demanding to see the mother abbess. 'Open the sanctuary!' the padre shouted as he pounded on the grilled door. A second later, the abbess appeared at the small window.

'Open this sanctuary?' she declared. Those sacred chambers had remained closed for more than seven hundred years. And they would not be opened now!

Leaving the mother abbess, the padre ran down the stairway and headed for the bishop's palace. Ducking down one alleyway and then another, he reached the palace and hurriedly told the *monsignore* what was happening. Together, the two worked their way towards the cloister, where the bishop ordered the abbess to open the sanctuary to let the Jews inside. Still she refused.

Suddenly they heard the march of heavy boots on the cobblestones of the piazza outside. Then the clanging of the huge iron gates as they were forced open. Orders were shouted and then the voice of

Sister Amata was heard as she struggled to keep her post at the little reception desk downstairs.

Hearing the commotion, at last the mother abbess turned the locks on the grilled door. One, then another, and then another, until finally the door swung open. The padre ran to the rooms where the Jews had gathered. Seeing the frantic warning on his face, they quickly followed him down the hallway toward the sanctuary. As the last Jew passed through the grilled door, it clanged shut, the bolts thrown into place. And the Sisters of Saint Clare renewed their sacred vows of secrecy and silence.

Since the day of the German occupation of Assisi, hundreds of fresh troops had arrived, taking their stations in and about town and setting up barricades at all points of entry. German officers were everywhere.

Throughout northern Italy, the Nazis continued to take control of villages, towns, and cities, and the hunt for Jews was their main objective. With each passing day, the numbers of Italian citizens, priests, and nuns involved in rescue efforts increased. In monasteries, convents, and homes, an estimated forty thousand Jews had found refuge from the enemy.

Padre Niccacci lost no time finding additional hiding places for the stream of refugees that were arriving in Assisi almost daily, disguising themselves as Catholics making pilgrimages to the holy city. The cloistered Sisters of Saint Colette and a group of German nuns who had once run a guest house had agreed to open their doors. And, in addition to a number of rooms at the seminary, there were numerous shrines and holy places dotting the hillsides outside of town that could provide shelter if the need arose.

For the moment, the most critical problem facing the padre was that of finding identification papers for refugees trying to escape from the country. Many church officials like Cardinal della Costa of Florence had organized rescue networks to transport hundreds of Jews to Switzerland and elsewhere. But proper identification papers were essential. Who in Assisi could provide those papers?

Late one November afternoon, as the padre finished his weekly game of draughts with Luigi Brizi, the idea came to him. Brizi was the perfect candidate. He was the finest engraver and printer in the whole of Umbria. The question was, would he do it? Would he be willing to take the risk? And could he be trusted?

Late that night, in the print shop on the Via Santa Chiara, Brizi and the padre sat hunched over a foot-operated press next to shelves filled with metal letter blocks.

The padre waited anxiously for Brizi to speak. Would he be able to copy the ID cards the bishop had collected from Catholic refugees now hiding in the palace? And what about the official government stamps and emblems?

The stamps and the wording of the IDs would be

no problem, Luigi said. But the engraving of provincial emblems would present a challenge. The work was so intricate, so fine. Rather like the engravings on the lire, which only a skilled counterfeiter could match. It would be difficult, the printer said. But it was worth the gamble. Luigi Brizi would enjoy making fools out of the Fascists.

Brizi went to work with zeal and energy. Hour after hour passed as he bent over his printer's blocks, adjusting the type, experimenting with a score of engravings, and holding his proofs to the light, looking for flaws that would fail close examination.

At last he was satisfied. Pulling a sample ID from the press, he studied it carefully, his skilled eye tracing each line, each curve and swirl, and then passed it to Niccacci. It was going to work.

With Brizi firmly committed to the task of producing the false identification papers, Niccacci organized a staff that would put the finishing touches on each one. Setting up quarters in the Cloister of the Sisters of Saint Clare, he enlisted the aid of several of the Jewish refugees. Within days after the printing of the first sample, hundreds of false papers had been issued, each bearing the genius of Luigi Brizi, master counterfeiter.

Toward the end of November, Padre Niccacci received a summons from Cardinal della Costa, Archbishop of Florence. Arriving in Florence early one morning, he was shocked by what he saw. Everywhere he looked, there were German troops, Gestapo, and SS units speeding down the streets on motorcycles, and armoured vans carrying screaming children. Loudspeakers shouted orders above the din of passing vehicles. *'Ach-tung! Attenzione!* Everyone out in the street! Carry nothing with you!'

As the padre walked to the cardinal's palace, he passed in front of a building surrounded by scores of SS and Gestapo officers. Seconds later, a number of Jewish men and women emerged from the entrance, pushed from behind by additional troops, their rifle butts buried in the backs of the prisoners. The last to leave was a priest.

Blindly, the padre pushed himself on towards the palace. Once inside, he was greeted by the cardinal's secretary, who was obviously distraught. The raid had come without warning and hundreds had been arrested. Cardinal della Costa had been trying to negotiate the release of some of the prisoners, but it was useless.

Niccacci told of what he had just witnessed, as the *monsignore* listened intently. Finally, he spoke.

The tall, young man with the heavy black beard that Padre Niccacci had seen being taken away by the Nazis must have been Nathan Cassuto, the chief rabbi of Florence; and the priest was Don Leto Casisi. They and the others were members of a group that had been active in finding hiding places for Jews.

Later that day, Cardinal della Costa returned, exhausted. More than one thousand men, women,

73

and children had been deported, he told Niccacci. And fifty of the orphans at the Convent of the Carmine Sisters ... had been taken. Only two little babies had been saved.

The rescue effort must continue, the bishop vowed to Niccacci. New escape routes must be established to replace those already sealed off. Cardinal della Costa told the padre he had seen Brizi's work several days before and was astounded by its quality. Jewish refugees from Perugia carrying Brizi's documents on their journey to Florence had passed through several checkpoints with no difficulty. They were now in hiding at the Monastery of San Marco.

As Cardinal della Costa saw it, Assisi was the perfect location for the centre of an underground counterfeiting network. With the proper identification papers, refugees could be smuggled through the town and across the front lines into Switzerland. Hundreds of lives could be saved.

Padre Niccacci thought for a moment. An undertaking such as this would require much planning and organizing. He would need more people to process the IDs, Brizi would have to have help, and they'd need to find more hiding places. Six of Assisi's monasteries had already opened their doors to the Jews, and twenty more in the area would have to be called upon to provide temporary shelter. But there was no choice.

Then the cardinal gave the padre some better news. Authorities at the Vatican had persuaded the Germans to turn Assisi into a hospital and rehabilitation facility for wounded Army officers. Stadtkommissar Stolmann would be replaced by a lieutenant colonel by the name of Valentin Müller. He was a Catholic. And a physician.

Lieutenant Colonel Müller arrived in Assisi two weeks before Christmas and immediately went about the reorganization of the Hotel Subasio into a convalescent hospital. Soon, he was a familiar face on Sunday mornings, attending mass at the Basilica of Saint Francis and later strolling through the streets of the town. The residents agreed that the new *commandante* was a great improvement over the last.

A steady stream of *pilgrims* now poured into Assisi by foot, arriving at night from hiding places in the surrounding mountains. As Niccacci had promised, monasteries throughout the area opened their doors to all who sought shelter. With each new group, the risk of discovery mounted. At any time, another raid could occur, monasteries and homes might be searched, and Brizi's counterfeit operation uncovered. With each passing day, the number of people aware of the underground activities grew, increasing the possibility of a slipup.

On Christmas Day, 1943, the colonel's limousine arrived at the Seminary of San Damiano with a large package for Padre Rufino Niccacci – a case of Moselle wine with a note wishing the padre a Merry Christmas and offering Colonel Müller's services if ever the need arose. And for the people of Assisi, he promised extra food rations to celebrate the holy season.

Within weeks of Colonel Müller's arrival, tensions

about the town eased, and the padre gave permission to those Jews who spoke Italian without accents to move about the area. With their new identification cards, the refugees were now free to acquire their own food rations, and many began attending mass on Sundays, having been coached by the padre to recite the prayers of the church. To the townspeople and the Germans alike, they were simply Catholic pilgrims from the south, seeking refuge in the holy city of Saint Francis.

On New Year's Day, Padre Niccacci was told by the bishop that a group of refugees was to be taken across the Sangro River, to an Allied encampment near Abruzzi. The group, travelling south from Florence, had been sent by the cardinal. The padre's assignment was to take them as far as the little village of Pescocostanzo, where they would be met by smugglers who would escort them across the river and into the safety of Allied hands.

At first, Niccacci refused. He wasn't a smuggler. He was a priest and a monk. And what about volunteers from Florence?

They had been caught, the bishop answered. Now the cardinal needed new people. And a different route.

Niccacci paced the floor. How would he transport these people? All trains to Abruzzi had been cancelled.

The padre would find a way, Bishop Nicolini answered.

Early the next morning, seventeen Jewish refugees

dressed in monks' robes climbed into a German military transport truck. With them, already in the front seat, sat Padre Rufino Niccacci, prayer book in hand. Next to him, a young German corporal waited at the wheel. The motor started, the doors clanged shut, and two German soldiers armed with rifles took their places in the rear. The padre managed a tense smile. The colonel's offer of assistance had not been forgotten.

After a journey of several hours, with Niccacci pulling out his rosary at each checkpoint, the truck carrying the seventeen *pilgrims* (one a Catholic priest) and three Germans arrived in Pescocostanzo. Pulling up to the door of a little church, the corporal parked, got out with the other soldiers, and started assisting everyone out of the truck. Suddenly, the corporal knelt before a rabbi dressed as a *monsignore*, bowed his head, and asked for a blessing. Startled, Padre Niccacci reached for his rosary once again and began fingering the beads. But the rabbi had done his homework. Without a change of expression, he held his hand over the corporal's head, made the sign of the cross, and said perfectly, 'I bless you, in the name of the Father, the Son, and the Holy Spirit.'

Moments later, the Germans drove off, promising to return the following morning to take the padre back to Assisi. A priest ushered the men into a room at the side of the church where a small meal had been prepared. Then, as they were eating, one of the smugglers appeared in the doorway and came towards them, demanding his money.

The padre was not pleased. To ensure the safety of his charges, he argued that the smugglers would receive their pay *after* the delivery of the refugees to the Allies.

But the smuggler was firm. The money, six thousand lire, paid in advance, or no trip.

The priest had money, but *not* six thousand lire! Just then, the vesper bells began to ring and people started filing into the church for mass. Suddenly Niccacci had an idea – he would take up a collection for the homeless war refugees.

Late that evening, having climbed a dark, winding path that led up into the mountains outside of town, the padre and the others followed Luigi and Vittorio, the two smugglers, to a forester's hut. There, the men warmed themselves before starting the long trek down the trail leading to the Sangro River. Luigi and Vittorio took their places in front of the group with two donkeys that would be used to carry food and provisions back from the Allies. The padre stayed behind in the hut to wait.

Hour after hour dragged by. Finally, towards dawn, the signal came. A single shot ringing out through the night. Vittorio and the Jewish refugees had made it!

The next afternoon, the padre returned to the seminary to find an SS officer pacing back and forth in front of the basilica. Introducing himself as Captain Ernst van den Velde, he explained that he had just been assigned the command of all security for the surrounding region and wanted to meet the civilian and religious leaders in the area.

Then refusing an offer of hospitality from the padre, the captain abruptly continued. Was the padre aware of the heavy smuggling taking place in the area? Merchandise. And people. Deserters, refugees from the north. And Jews. Niccacci shrugged. How would *he* know about such things?

Van den Velde issued his parting comment. All routes leading in and out of Assisi would be closely watched. There would be no further escapes and no new *pilgrims* seeking the holy shrines of Saint Francis.

During the weeks that followed, the weather turned bitter cold. The stream of refugees to the holy shrines diminished to a trickle after the closing of a number of routes to the north and south.

One day, an underground scout on a mission to Pescocostanzo returned with tragic news. In a surprise raid by the Gestapo, Luigi, the smuggler, had been shot and killed, and the old forester captured and sent to a concentration camp. Only Vittorio had escaped. The final road to freedom had been clamped shut, just as van den Velde had promised.

A short time later, four of the Jewish refugees from the San Damiano Seminary were arrested while transporting counterfeit identification cards to Perugia. Interrogated and tortured, they refused to break, revealing nothing about the activities of the Assisi underground.

Late one night, as the padre returned by foot from a visit with his family in Deruta, he found Captain van den Velde's Volkswagen in the seminary driveway. It was time for a little drive, the captain said with an artificial smile. Perhaps the padre would be interested in a tour of the Gestapo headquarters at Bastia.

After relentless questioning in van den Velde's office, Padre Niccacci was taken to a tiny medieval cell in the basement of the Bastia headquarters. The area was cold, dank, and foul-smelling. A narrow cot was against the stone wall. In the corner was a tin bucket. Above, a light shone from a bare bulb in the ceiling.

For days, Padre Niccacci remained in this cell. He was denied food and water, and the heavy bars and the door in front of them remained locked. Outside in the courtyard, he could hear the rhythmic steps of guards pacing back and forth, and occasionally the sound of a Gestapo van entering or leaving the prison. The light above his cot stayed on day and night, making it impossible to sleep.

Late one night, Niccacci heard his name shouted and saw the bolts to the cell door turning one by one. In an instant, a guard was by his cot, a rifle butt in his back. 'Move!' the guard ordered.

In the courtyard outside, a truck waited, and the padre and a number of other prisoners were hustled on board. Dazed, hungry, and weak he clutched the side of the truck to steady himself, for there was no room to sit down. And then he heard the word he most dreaded. Perugia. He was going to be executed.

Shortly after five o'clock the next morning, the truck pulled into Carcere Femminile, a former women's prison. Padre Niccacci stared incredulously at the scene before him. Here in the walled courtyard of an ancient prison, the condemned waited to die. Five at a time, the men were shoved against the side of the building, the order given, the shots fired. The words of the Requiem passed his lips. And then, the mercy of darkness.

Minutes later, the padre found himself in an interrogation room with van den Velde shouting at him. Was he going to confess at last? Through the door came two emaciated prisoners. Niccacci looked into their hollow eyes, barely recognizing the Jewish refugees, Paolo Jozsa and Giorgio Kropf. The padre asked for water but it was denied. And then the interrogations resumed.

Hours later, the padre opened his eyes to find a nun standing by his cot. In her hands he saw a glass of milk and a small bowl of soup. Sitting down beside him, the woman held the glass while he drank. Then she fed him the soup, spoonful by spoonful.

Shortly after, a man entered the cell, introducing himself as a lawyer who had come to defend him. A trial, Niccacci mused. Why not just get on with the execution?

The lawyer began to explain. A close friend in Assisi had asked him to intervene in the padre's case because of his connections with Field-Marshal

Kesselring, the Supreme Commander of German occupational forces in Italy. Would the padre know his friend, perhaps? The former mayor of Assisi, Arnaldo Fortini?

It was some time before the priest could comprehend the lawyer's words. His head and body ached with the events of the past weeks. What about Paolo and Giorgio and the others? And the refugees in Assisi. What had become of them after his arrest?

Paolo's and Giorgio's papers were in the hands of the German chief judge for the province of Perugia, the lawyer said. Perhaps, there wouldn't be a trial at all.

Later that day, Padre Niccacci walked out into the clean fresh air of a winter's day. Frail, drawn, and looking much older than his years, he was nevertheless a free man. Once more, he offered his silent thanksgiving for the Lord's grace. His lawyer was Barone Vincenzo Texeira, a man of professional prestige and of a noble Italian family. He was indeed 'well-connected' and was working with men of influence, Germans in high places. They were eager to save their skins the moment armistice was declared, for it became clearer with each passing day that the Third Reich was losing ground.

The grey days of a northern Italian winter gave way at last to spring. After mass each morning, Padre Niccacci took his hourly stroll along the cloistered garden of the Seminary of San Damiano. It had been a long time since he had walked to Assisi. After Don Brunacci's warning of van den Velde's determination to flush out the Assisi underground, he had stayed at the seminary, relying on visitors to keep him informed of the refugees.

It was on a stroll such as this that the priest was startled one morning to hear the rumble of a military Volkswagen as it crossed the pebbled driveway leading to the seminary's entrance. Certain that it was van den Velde, Niccacci expected the worst.

The car door opened and slammed shut, and the young driver, wearing the black armband of an interpreter for the German Command in Perugia, ran toward the cloister. It was Giorgio!

Barone Texeira had lost no time in pressing the German chief judge to act on the cases of the four Jewish refugees. In a review of the files, a decision was made that all evidence against the men would be dropped. Learning that Giorgio and Paolo spoke German with ease, the judge had decided that they could be useful. The two men were now interpreters at the German army headquarters in Perugia.

Late in April, Paolo Jozsa returned to the seminary with a surprise for the padre. Using his influence at German headquarters, he had gained access to some blank official papers, stamped with the official seal of the Supreme Commander, Field-Marshal Kesselring. Drawing upon his experiences in working with Brizi's counterfeit IDs, Paolo had typed a forged edict declaring Assisi an open city. Evacuation of all German tanks, artillery, and military personnel was to take effect immediately.

On 17 June 1944, Padre Niccacci and the brothers

of the sacred Seminary of San Damiano awakened early to the roar of tanks moving in the direction of Assisi. Grabbing their robes, the men ran downstairs and out to the highway. The tanks were coming from the south, and with ordered precision were inching their way toward the hilltown. Two weeks before, on 4 June, the Allies had liberated Rome. Less than forty-eight hours later, the invasion of Normandy had begun. And now, Assisi.

As if on cue, church bells began to ring. Soon, the entire area was echoing with the bells of all the sacred shrines.

And then, from the houses and convents and monasteries throughout the town, the people came, with armloads of flowers and loaves of bread for the advancing troops. And from their hiding places poured the Jewish refugees. The British had arrived in Assisi.

Throngs of people were moving towards the centre of the town and the priests of San Damiano joined with them. Entering the Basilica of Saint Francis, Padre Niccacci and the others heard a new sound rising above the roar of the tanks and the bells. Music, coming from the second floor. In the organ loft, with the basilica's loudspeakers turned on for all the town to hear, sat Maestro Fano, his yarmulke on his head and his monk's robes billowing out behind him, playing 'God Save the King', the British national anthem.

6
'Look at Your Feet and Keep on Walking!'

Madame Marie

Odette Meyers was seven years old when the Germans began their round-up of almost 13,000 Jews in Paris on 16 July 1942. A pretty little girl with thick, wavy black hair and inquiring eyes, Odette was the only child of working-class parents who had emigrated from Poland during the 1920s.

At the time of the round-up, Odette and her mother were living in an apartment in a building run by a woman known as Madame Marie. Although the Meyers family was Jewish and Marie and her husband were Catholic, a friendship had developed, particularly after Odette's father had been captured

85

by the Germans and the mother and child were left alone.

Early on the morning of the raid, Madame Marie heard the rumbling of German trucks and the screams of Jewish neighbours being taken from their homes. Running upstairs to warn Odette and her mother about what was happening, she ordered the two to follow her to her own apartment, and hurriedly shoved them into a broom closet seconds before the Germans appeared at her door.

With no time to lose, Marie greeted the soldiers with a flourish of hospitality, uncorking a bottle of wine and showing them to her kitchen table. As the search team emptied their glasses, the Frenchwoman thanked them repeatedly for their actions in getting rid of the Jews and pretended to be grateful for what they were doing.

While Odette and her mother huddled in the tiny closet, Marie poured a second glass of wine for the Germans who, by now, had started asking questions about the two Jews they had come to arrest. Marie responded with a stream of anti-Semitic insults about Odette and her mother. And all the while, she continued to pour the wine.

Then, one of the Germans began threatening Madame Marie and demanded to see the Meyers' apartment. Flying into a tirade, Marie insisted that they would not want to step into such a filthy place. And besides, she grumbled, the Meyers had left for a vacation in the country, something she herself couldn't possibly afford.

As the last of the wine was emptied, the Germans staggered to the door and left. Marie listened as the soldiers moved on down the hallway and then ran to the phone to call her husband, Henri. Like Odette's mother and many others, Henri was active in the French Resistance and had helped many Jews find safety in the countryside. Hurrying home from his job, Henri told Odette to follow him immediately.

Outside on the street, the Germans were everywhere. Henri held Odette's trembling hand while the two passed a line of trucks filled with captured Jews.

'Look at your feet and keep on walking!' the tall Frenchman whispered to the little girl. And so the two continued, until they reached a deserted subway that led them to the main railway out of Paris.

Odette Meyers spent the duration of the war in hiding, passing as a Catholic child and attending a convent school in a small French village. Marie and Henri found hiding places for many other Jews.

After the German defeat, Odette and her mother were reunited and eventually went to the United States. A university professor and a poet, Odette now lives in Berkeley, California, grateful to Madame Marie for saving her life – and her spirit also.

Irene

Irene Opdyke was a young nursing student when the German army marched into Poland in 1939. For three weeks, stretchers carrying wounded Polish soldiers filed past her in the crowded wards of the hospital where she worked. Then, with the collapse of the military, Poland fell to the Germans. Irene's hospital was evacuated and villages in the surrounding area were occupied by the enemy.

Joining the army in the hope that her nursing skills would be useful on the battlefield, the young girl soon found herself on the run as pockets of the military fought against the German onslaught. Escaping into a forest that bordered the then-Soviet Ukraine, she and a small band of soldiers and nurses started the Polish underground. Weeks passed and the number of freedom fighters increased. Hiding out in the forest by day and moving into villages at night to launch raids on the Germans, Irene was often left to guard an area while others in her group searched for food.

One night, as Irene stood watch, a truckload of Soviet soldiers rumbled into town and headed in her direction. Suddenly, the soldiers began jumping off the truck and running toward her. Irene raced for the forest, but the men quickly overtook her. In an instant, they knocked the young woman to the ground, where she was beaten and left by the roadside.

Hours later, Irene awoke to find herself in a Soviet

prison hospital, tended by a woman doctor who treated her wounds and offered her compassion and understanding. When Irene had recovered, the doctor assigned her to nursing duties, where she worked long hours in wards filled with disease but little medicine to treat the wounded.

In 1941, the Germans and the Soviets exchanged prisoners and Irene was sent back to German-occupied Poland to an area that was within a short distance of her family's home. On her way to the village where she hoped to find her parents, the young woman stopped into a little church to attend mass.

Suddenly, the church was surrounded by Germans and everyone inside was rounded up. A prisoner once again, Irene was assigned to a munitions factory that was located next to a walled-off Jewish ghetto.

One morning, as her group was being transported to the factory, Irene and the others saw a long trail of Jews on a forced march from the ghetto. Gestapo guards were shouting orders to the sick and the elderly, kicking and shoving rifle butts into those who couldn't keep pace. Irene watched as an old rabbi, clutching his Torah, hobbled alongside a woman in the final months of pregnancy. Children screamed and clung to their mothers' skirts. Later that day, Irene discovered what had happened to the people. Walking to the centre of the town, she found masses of open graves filled with bodies. As she moved along the graves, she made a vow that she would find a way to help the Jews of the ghetto.

A short time later, the chance to help came. Transferred to the officers' dining rooms, Irene soon met twelve Jewish men and women who had been ordered to work in the laundry rooms. She could see that they were half-starved and exhausted from long hours of labour, so she began smuggling bits of bread and other leftovers out of the dining rooms. From time to time, Irene passed information to the Jews from conversations she had overheard.

Eventually, Irene and the Jews formed a news network that warned people in the ghetto about scheduled raids, allowing them time to find a way to hide. Soon, more than three hundred Jews had managed to escape. Angered, the Germans ordered the liquidation of the ghetto and deportations to the death camps began.

Irene was afraid for her Jewish friends, but felt powerless to help. What could she do?

And then one day, an elderly major she had waited on in the dining rooms asked her if she would become his housekeeper. Irene accepted the offer and immediately sent word to the Jews that she would leave a basement window in the major's villa open for them. Soon, one by one, her friends arrived.

For three years, Irene acted as a housekeeper for the major, hiding the Jews in the coal room of the cellar and supplying them with food from upstairs. And then, one day, it happened.

On a trip to the village to do errands for the

major, Irene and a number of other people were rounded up by the local Gestapo and ordered to watch the hangings of several Polish families and the Jews they had been hiding.

Some time later, Irene was allowed to return to the villa, but she was so upset that she forgot to leave the key in the door so that, if the major returned suddenly, he would not be able to open it himself. Walking to the kitchen, she found four of the Jewish women who frequently came upstairs to help her when the German was away.

Suddenly, the front door opened and the major walked in. Seeing Irene and the others, the officer was outraged.

How could she do this? Did she know what could happen to her? Yes, Irene answered, she had just been to the village. But no one had the right to murder because of someone's religion or race. And these people were her friends.

Moments went by. Finally, the major spoke. He could not do that to her, he said. He couldn't just let her die after all she had done for him.

Falling to her knees, Irene grabbed the German's hand and kissed it. Not for herself, she would say many years later, but for the Jews of the villa and for all the people in hiding who depended on her.

Weeks later, with the Germans in retreat, the major deserted the villa, leaving Irene and her friends behind. Together, they waited for the war to end, moving into the Ukrainian forest and offering aid to Jews and freedom fighters who needed them. When the Russians moved in, the Jews were freed and Irene was sent to a displaced persons camp. In 1949, she came to the United States and settled in California. But she never lost touch with her Jewish friends.

Not long ago, Irene was asked what lessons could be learned from what she had done.

We must teach that we belong together, she said. We all live by one God. . . .

John

John Weidner grew up in the little French village of Collonges, close to the Swiss border. His father was a minister of the Seventh Day Adventist Church and taught Latin and Greek at the local academy.

In the home where John and his older sister, Gabrielle, grew up, prejudice against Jews was not permitted. The children were taught the words of the Hebrew prophets and were often reminded that Christ himself was a Jew.

After graduation from the University of Geneva, John moved to Paris, where he went into business for himself. Then, in June of 1940, the Germans took control of France and began their persecution of the Jews.

One day, while waiting for a train, John Weidner saw a group of women and children who were being deported to the camps. In the confusion, a baby began to cry. One of the soldiers guarding the Jews ordered the infant's mother to make it stop crying. Then, suddenly, he reached out for the child and threw it to the station floor.

Some time later, John returned to his family home in Collonges determined to find a way to smuggle Jews across the border and into Switzerland, a neutral country. Working by himself at first, he soon found he needed the help of his parents and his sister, Gabrielle. Soon, he had built an underground organization that became known as Dutch-Paris. John and Gabrielle headed the group, working out an escape route through Holland and Belgium, and onto France and Switzerland.

Eventually, the sister-and-brother team had nearly three hundred volunteers, each with assignments so dangerous that only the barest facts were known to anyone.

John and Gabrielle faced enormous hazards in their rescue efforts. Travel was a problem during the cold winter months, and hiding places along the network of stations leading from one country to another had to be changed frequently to avoid discovery. John's old school in Collonges became the last stopover before the escape into Switzerland, and he and the others often had to cross on skis. Then there was the problem of raising enough money for bribes and false identification papers.

One night, a young woman working with the rescuers was captured. Arrested, interrogated, and tortured, the woman broke down, confessing the names of one hundred and fifty people in the underground. All were arrested and shipped to concentration camps. Gabrielle was among those who never returned.

A short time after, John was arrested and sentenced to death. On the day before his execution, one of John's guards noticed a small, pocket-sized Bible in his jacket. Taking the young prisoner to the third floor, the guard pointed to a small window that overlooked a hidden courtyard. John jumped, landing uninjured on the ground below. Moving quickly into a thick stand of trees, he found his way to a friend's home. Later, with the help of the French underground, John reached London and met with the Allied Command to plan the rescue of more than two hundred Allied soldiers and airmen in Europe.

Despite the loss of so many people, the members of Dutch-Paris continued their work until the end of the war. John is modest about the work he did. In a recent film about the rescuers, John said that the most important thing in life is to have a heart that is open to the sufferings of others.

Germaine, Liliane, and François

Germaine Belline was a young mother when the German Army marched into Belgium in May of 1940. During the early months of the occupation, her husband was taken prisoner and shipped to Germany, leaving Germaine to carry on the family's tailoring shop in La Louvière, a factory town thirty miles southwest of Brussels.

By 1941, the Nazis had begun the deportation of Belgian Jews to the camps of Eastern Europe. And it was during this time that a town house in the middle of La Louvière became a haven of rescue.

The first to arrive at the Belline home were two orphaned Jewish boys. Later, Germaine took in other Jews. Once, when friends learned that they were about to be arrested, Germaine supplied them with false ID papers, ration cards, and a hiding place. Elza, the couple's only child, went into hiding in the Belline home.

Soon, Germaine was protecting and feeding thirty-one Jewish refugees with the help of her daughter, Liliane, and her son, François. During this time, food was scarce and the round-ups of the Jews in La Louvière increased.

Late in the war, Germaine's husband, Charles, escaped from the German prison camp and became an officer in the Belgian underground.

Until the end of the war, Liliane and her brother, François, worked in countless rescue efforts with their parents, smuggling guns, food, and false IDs to Jews in hiding. Often, they played with children of Nazi sympathizers, so that their underground activities would not be suspected. At night, they frequently led Jewish refugees to hiding places in remote villages outside of town.

Each evening, the people of La Louvière would drape their windows with heavy, black air raid blankets. In the Belline home, this was the signal for silent games with the Jewish refugees and a chance for hushed conversation.

There were many crises during those years. Two babies were born, with Germaine and the other women acting as midwives, since no doctor could be called to the house. And there was the evening when three German soldiers on patrol suddenly burst into the Bellines' living room. Germaine startled the soldiers by lifting up her skirt, making it look like she was dressing. The embarrassed soldiers made a fast retreat. Liliane was once arrested by the Gestapo and questioned, but her quick-witted answers finally led to her release.

After the war, the Belline family moved to the United States, but they continued their friendship with the refugees. François, once an eight-year-old smuggler of guns and Jews, became an ace test pilot. Liliane is now a languages professor at a New Jersey university. Of the family's wartime activities, she has said that their mother didn't give them any choice. They were simply told not to tell a soul about what the Bellines were doing.

Willy

By September of 1944, Germany was suffering heavy losses, not only on its Eastern European Front but at home as well. With millions of young men on the battlefields, there was a desperate need for workers in the industrial plants and munitions factories. Trains began arriving from Auschwitz and other concentration camps, loaded with prisoners who were immediately put to work. Most of these were lame, sick, and half-starved. Ray Kaner was among them.

After five years of starvation and disease, the

young seventeen-year-old girl was so thin that her stunted growth made her look like a small child. When she arrived in Hambieren, Germany, she was ordered to a construction site, loading heavy sacks onto wagons and hauling equipment up steep hills and down into ravines that were full of mud and garbage.

One evening, after Ray returned to her prison block, a sixty-year-old guard named Willy Minke took pity on her and left his post to smuggle food from the officers' dining room. Returning to Ray's barracks, he located the young girl and offered her the food. Then, while Willy stood guard at the window, Ray crawled under her cot and ate.

As the months wore on, food at the Hambieren camp grew scarce. Despite this, Willy continued to smuggle scraps of leftovers from the dining room. Soon, he found lighter work for Ray in the officers' barracks.

In January of 1945, the prisoners of Hambieren were marched to the Bergen-Belsen concentration camp, and Willy was ordered to go with them. Arriving in Belsen, he found conditions to be the worst he had seen. Soon, Willy and Ray, along with the others, were stricken with typhus and dysentery. During the time that they were ill, the two lost contact with each other.

Finally, in April of 1945, Bergen-Belsen was liberated by the Allies. Ray was among the survivors.

After months in a hospital, Ray Kaner located her friend, Willy, and his wife. She discovered that Willy had been arrested during the liberation, but was later released on the testimony of other Jewish prisoners he had helped.

Willy and his wife continued their friendship with Ray Kaner long after she had emigrated to America, a friendship that lasted until Willy's death.

Jonka

Jonka Kowalyk still finds it hard to talk about her activities during the war. Remembering how afraid everyone was, she adds that there was never a time when they weren't waiting to be arrested.

Jonka had good reason to be scared. From 1942 until 1944, she and her widowed mother hid fourteen Ukrainian Jews in the attic of their home in a small farming village that bordered a Nazi labour camp.

One of ten children, Jonka worked as a seamstress, making barely enough money to pay for food for herself and her mother. Often, as she sat at her window, she would see the lines of Jewish prisoners as they were marched to and from their worksites. Jonka smuggled food into the camp when she could. One time, she was shot in the leg by an SS guard who had warned her to stay away.

When Jonka's mother became very ill, she walked back to the camp to persuade a German officer to send an inmate doctor to her mother's bedside. When the Jewish physician arrived, he treated the mother and then begged Jonka to find him a hiding place. Without stopping to think about the consequences, Jonka told the prisoner that, if he could find a way to escape, she would hide him in the attic of her home.

Several weeks later, the prisoner, Dr Solomon Berger, and thirteen other inmates, escaped from the camp while it was being liquidated and the inmates deported. Unable to turn the people away, Jonka and her mother found room for all of them in the attic of their little cottage. That night, as deportation lines passed in front of the Kowalyk home, Jonka ran out and grabbed a three-year-old child, taking him to Kraków to stay with a relative of hers.

During the two years that the Jews were in hiding, there were constant dangers. Gestapo patrols often moved through the village and carried out inspections. Suspicious neighbours sent the secret police to check on the Kowalyks' activities. More than once, Jonka and her group owed their lives to an old mandolin and a wooden flute. Keeping the instruments close at hand, the woman would run into her garden whenever the Nazis approached and begin playing. The music distracted the patrols and signalled the Jews upstairs to find places to hide.

There were other threats. Once, as the Germans broke into the attic seconds after the Jews had escaped to an underground bunker beneath the house, they found a dish of freshly snuffed-out cigarettes and a set of playing cards. Jonka's nine-year-old nephew, who had followed the soldiers upstairs and who knew of the conspiracy, tugged on the arm of an officer.

'Don't tell my mother,' the boy whispered frantically. '*She'll kill me!*' he said, explaining that he and several friends often hid in the attic to smoke and gamble in secrecy. The child was so convincing that the officer believed his story and called off the search.

As the weeks and months dragged on, Jonka and her mother faced one crisis after another. When one of the Jews became ill and died, there was the question of how to dispose of the body. Another time, one of the children crept out of the house to play with some children, and told them where she lived. Always, the simplest duties were difficult to carry out. Chamber pots and garbage had to be removed every day, and medicines had to be found for people who became sick.

Through it all, Jonka and her mother continued their work. Jonka made clothes for the people and shared her meagre food rations with them, often going hungry so that they might eat.

After the war, Jonka received an anonymous letter threatening her life and warning her to leave the country. No longer safe, she left her family and went to the United States. For a short time, she was married to Dr Berger, the physician who had treated her mother. But the marriage didn't last and Jonka was alone once again.

Eventually, Jonka Kowalyk found work as a seamstress in New York, saving bus fare by walking two hours each day to and from work so that she could send money to her family in Russia each month. Later she skipped meals in order to bring her young nephew and his wife to America. This was the same nephew who had once bravely fooled the German officer on the day of the raid.

When it came to helping others, Jonka Kowalyk always found a way.

Epilogue

Philip P. Hallie, author of *Lest Innocent Blood Be Shed*, the story of the rescuers of Le Chambon, wrote:

> Rescue is not always accompanied by blazing guns and blaring bugles. Sometimes the quiet kind can be just as effective – and just as dangerous.

When we think of the quiet courage of Miep and Henk Gies, the people of Le Chambon, and all the others who refused to turn their backs on the Jews of the Holocaust, we ask ourselves how it happened that these few men, women, and children gathered the strength to face the risks they had to take. Who were the rescuers, why did they do what they did?

Nechama Tec, a well-known sociologist and herself a hidden child, suggests that the Holocaust rescuers were people who acted out of a deep moral conviction to respond to the suffering of another human being. Because of this conviction, the rescuers did what their consciences told them they had to do. And because of these singular acts of goodness, more than two million people were saved from the gas chambers.

During the years following the war, many rescuers did not want their identities known, particularly in countries where anti-Semitism was strong. Rescuers were often thrown into jail, shot by a neighbour, or simply disappeared. Many, like Oskar Schindler and Hermann Graebe (the only German to testify against the Nazis at the Nuremberg trials) were forced to leave the country.

Elie Wiesel, a survivor of the camps and a winner of the Nobel Peace Prize, talks of the moral obligation to protect the welfare and the rights of others:

> Let us not forget, after all, that there is always the moment when the moral choice is made. Often it is because of . . . one person (that) we are able to make a different choice, a choice for humanity, for life. And so we must know these good people who helped Jews during the Holocaust. We must learn from them, and in gratitude, we must remember them.

Bibliography

Books

Anger, Per. *With Raoul Wallenberg in Budapest.* New York: The Holocaust Library, 1981.

Berg, Mary. *Warsaw Ghetto: A Diary.* New York: L. B. Fischer, 1945.

Eisenberg, Azreil. *The Lost Generation: Children of the Holocaust.* New York, Pilgrim Press, 1982.

Frank, Anne. *Anne Frank: The Diary of a Young Girl.* New York: Simon and Schuster, 1952.

Friedman, Philip, *Their Brothers' Keepers.* New York: The Holocaust Library, 1978.

Gies, Miep. *Anne Frank Remembered.* New York: Simon and Schuster, 1987.

Hallie, Philip. *Lest Innocent Blood Be Shed.* New York: Harper and Row, 1979.

Huneke, Douglas. *The Moses of Rovno*. New York: Dodd Mead and Company, 1985.

Keneally, Thomas. *Schindler's List*. New York: Penguin, 1983.

Meltzer, Milton. *Never to Forget*. New York: Harper and Row, 1976.

Ramati, Alexander. *The Assisi Underground*. New York: Stein and Day, 1978.

Rittner, Carol, and Sondra Meyer, eds. *The Courage to Care*. New York: University Press, 1986.

Sim, Kevin. *Women at War: Five Who Defied the Nazis*. New York: William Morrow, 1982.

Stadtler, Bea. *The Holocaust: A History of Courage and Resistance*. New York: Behrman House, 1975.

Tec, Nechama. *Dry Tears: The Story of a Lost Childhood*. New York: Oxford University Press, 1984.

Valavkova, Hana. *I Never Saw Another Butterfly*. New York: Schoken Books, 1964.

Vegh, Claudine. *I Didn't Say Goodbye: Interviews with Children of the Holocaust*. New York: E. P. Dutton, 1979.

Weinstein, Frida. *A Hidden Childhood*. New York: Hill and Young, 1985.

Zuccotti, Susan. *The Italians and the Holocaust*. New York: Basic Books, 1987.

Papers, Pamphlets, Articles

Goldman, Ari. 'A Yeshiva Honors a Japanese Protector'. *The New York Times*: 21 April 1991.

'Human Relations Materials for the School'. New York: Anti-Defamation League, 1989. Films, books, video-cassettes, materials.

Levenson, Debbie. 'What Motivated the Heroes of the Holocaust'. *Boston Jewish Advocate*: 20 September 1990.

'Moral Courage during the Holocaust'. New York: Jewish

Foundation for Christian Rescuers/Anti-Defamation League: May 1990.

Schlegel, Sharon. 'Anton Suchinsky – Portrait of a Hero'. Trenton Times: 15 February 1991.

Sonnensheim, Frances, Ed. D. 'A Short History of Anti-Semitism.' New York: Jewish Foundation for Christian Rescuers/Anti-Defamation League: 1990.

'The Stories of Four Christian Rescuers and Why They Need Our Help.' New York: Jewish Foundation for Christian Rescuers/Anti-Defamation League: May 1990.

Index

112

Picture credits

Pages 1, 4 (bottom), and 5 courtesy of UPI/Bettmann. Page 2 (bottom) courtesy of Anne-Marie O'Healy. Pages 2 (top), and 3 courtesy of AP/Wide World. Pages 4 (top) and 7 (bottom) courtesy of Yad Vashem, Jerusalem, Israel. Page 6 Courtesy of N. Trocme Hewett/Swathmore College Peace Collection. Page 7 (top) courtesy of the Leo Baeck Institute, New York. Page 8 (top and bottom) courtesy of the Centre for Holocaust Studies, Museum of Jewish Heritage, New York. Additional thanks to Anne Frank Stichting for permission to use the images of Anne Frank's house, Anne Frank's handwriting, Anne Frank and Miep Gies.
© AFF/AFS Amsterdam, The Netherlands.